Hacking with Linux: Master the Basics of Kali for Ethical Hacking and Cybersecurity

Marco Luis

This book is intended for educational purposes only. The author and publisher do not condone or encourage illegal activities. Readers are encouraged to use the knowledge gained responsibly and ethically.

Table of Contact

Contents

Introduction: Your Journey into Linux-Powered Hacking 7

Chapter 1: Linux Foundations 10

- 1.1 What is Linux? (History, Open Source) 10
- 1.2 Understanding the Linux Kernel and Distributions: Separating the Core from the Package 12
- 1.3 Introduction to Kali Linux: Purpose & Philosophy: More Than Just a Collection of Tools 15
- 1.4 Navigating the Kali Desktop Environment: Getting Around Like a Pro 18
- 1.5 Basic Command Line Operations: ls, cd, pwd, mkdir, rm: Your First Steps to Command-Line Mastery 21

Chapter 2: Mastering the Command Line: Beyond the Basics 25

- 2.1 File System Navigation & Manipulation: Becoming a File System Ninja 25
- 2.2 Working with Files: cat, less, head, tail, grep, find: Unveiling the Secrets Within 30
- 2.3 Redirection & Piping: Combining Commands for Maximum Power: Unleash the Command-Line Symphony 35
- 2.4 User Accounts & Permissions: Securing Your System 39
- 2.5 Package Management (apt): Installing, Updating, and Removing Software: Your Gateway to the Software Universe 42

Chapter 3: Networking Essentials: Connecting the Dots in the Digital World 47

- 3.1 Networking Fundamentals: IP Addresses, Subnets, DNS: Laying the Foundation for Network Mastery 48
- 3.2 Network Protocols: TCP/IP, HTTP, SSH: Understanding the Conversation 54
- 3.3 Network Configuration: ifconfig / ip, Configuration Files: Making the Connection 59
- 3.4 Common Network Tools: ping, traceroute, netstat / ss: Become a Network Detective 65
- 3.5 Understanding Network Services & Ports: The Keys to the Kingdom 70

Chapter 4: Network Scanning & Reconnaissance: Gathering Intelligence Like a Pro 75

- 4.1 Introduction to Network Scanning: Mapping Out the Territory 76

4.2 Nmap: Host Discovery, Port Scanning, Service Detection: Your Swiss Army Knife for Network Exploration 78

4.3 Advanced Nmap Techniques: OS Detection, Version Scanning: Digging Deeper for Hidden Clues....83

4.4 Packet Sniffing: Wireshark / tcpdump Basics: Listening to the Network's Secrets......89

4.5 Passive Reconnaissance: Gathering Intelligence From the Shadows 93

Chapter 5: Bash Scripting for Hackers: Automating Your Way to Victory....98

5.1 Introduction to Bash Scripting: Shebang, Execution: Hello, World! (The Hacking Edition) 98

5.2 Variables, Data Types, Operators: Giving Your Scripts the Power to Remember and Calculate 102

5.3 Conditional Statements: if, then, else, elif, fi: Giving Your Scripts the Power to Think 107

5.4 Loops: for, while, until: Unleashing the Power of Repetition 113

5.5 Functions: Creating Reusable Code: Building Blocks for Scripting Mastery 119

Chapter 6: Automating Hacking Tasks with Scripts: Putting Your Skills to Work....123

6.2 Scripting for Password Cracking (Dictionary Attacks): Automating the Guessing Game 126

6.3 Log Analysis & Event Detection Scripts: Finding Needles in Haystacks of Data 129

List of log files to analyze....133

Search pattern....133

Loop through each log file 133

6.4 Automating Repetitive Tasks: Tying It All Together - Building Your Custom Workflow 135

Chapter 7: Basic Exploitation Concepts: Understanding the Attacker's Mindset....138

7.1 Introduction to Vulnerabilities and Exploits: Seeing the World Through an Attacker's Eyes (Ethically!)....139

7.2 Brute-Forcing SSH Logins: A Hands-On Example (Ethical Hacking Only!)....142

7.3 Exploiting a Basic Vulnerable Web Application (SQLi, XSS - Conceptual): A Window into Web Security....146

7.4 Introduction to Metasploit (Brief Overview, No Deep Dive): The Hacker's Toolkit on Steroids....151

Chapter 8: System Hardening & Security Best Practices: Building a Fortress 156

8.1 Secure Password Management: The First Line of Defense - Defending the Gate 156

8.2 User Account Security: Limiting Privileges - The Principle of Least Privilege 160

8.3 Firewall Configuration (ufw / iptables Basics): Guarding the Gates - Your Network Traffic Cop 164

8.4 Keeping Your System Updated: Patching Vulnerabilities - Staying Ahead of the Curve 167

8.5 Disabling Unnecessary Services: Shrinking the Target - Minimizing Your Exposure 171

8.6 Introduction to Intrusion Detection: Setting Up the Alarm System 174

Chapter 9: Web Application Security Basics: Defending the Digital Facade....................179

9.1 Common Web Vulnerabilities: SQL Injection, XSS, CSRF (Conceptual): Peering into the Web Security Abyss 179

9.2 Web Application Security Testing Techniques: Becoming a Web Application Detective 182

9.3 Introduction to OWASP Top Ten: Your Guide to the Web Security Hotlist 186

9.4 Secure Coding Practices: Building Defenses into the Code 189

Chapter 10: Cryptography Fundamentals: Securing Data with Secret Codes 193

10.1 Hashing Algorithms: Creating Unique Fingerprints - The One-Way Street of Data Security 193

10.2 Symmetric Encryption: The Secret Key - Keeping Secrets with Shared Knowledge 197

10.3 Asymmetric Encryption: The Public Key Advantage - Sharing Secrets Without Sharing the Key 200

10.4 Digital Signatures: Verifying Authenticity - Your Seal of Approval in the Digital World 204

10.5 Using GPG for Encryption & Signing: Securing Your Digital Life, One Key at a Time 207

Introduction: Your Journey into Linux-Powered Hacking

So, you're thinking about hacking? Excellent! But hold on a second. Forget the Hollywood images of rapid-fire keystrokes and instantly compromised systems. Real hacking, *ethical* hacking, is a lot more about careful planning, methodical execution, and a deep understanding of the systems you're trying to assess. And that's where Linux comes in.

Why Linux Matters for Hackers:

Think of Linux as the ultimate toolbox for anyone serious about cybersecurity. It's not just an operating system; it's an ecosystem of tools, a philosophy of openness, and a culture of sharing knowledge. There are a few crucial reasons why Linux dominates the hacking world:

- **Open-Source Power:** Linux is open source, which means its source code is freely available for anyone to inspect, modify, and redistribute. This transparency is a game-changer. Hackers can (and do) pore over the code, finding vulnerabilities that might be hidden in proprietary systems.
- **Command-Line Control:** Linux puts you in direct control through its command line. While graphical interfaces are fine for everyday tasks, the command line is where you unleash the real power. It lets you automate tasks, manipulate files, and interact with the system at a very granular level.
- **Customization is Key:** Linux is incredibly customizable. You can tailor it precisely to your needs, adding or removing tools, tweaking configurations, and optimizing performance. This flexibility is invaluable for hackers who need a system that can adapt to any situation.
- **The Toolset:** Countless security tools are built specifically for Linux. Tools like Nmap, Wireshark, Metasploit, and countless others are all readily available and deeply integrated into the Linux environment.

Ethical Hacking & Cybersecurity: Scope and Legality:

Let's get one thing crystal clear: this book focuses on **ethical hacking**. That means you'll learn to use hacking techniques to identify vulnerabilities in systems *with permission* from the owner. This is crucial. Unauthorized access to computer systems is illegal and can have severe consequences.

Ethical hacking is also known as penetration testing or security auditing. Professionals in this field are hired to assess the security posture of organizations, finding weaknesses before malicious actors can exploit them. It's a vital part of cybersecurity and a growing field with high demand.

We will explore the boundaries between ethical and unethical hacking in the context of applicable laws.

Setting Up Your Hacking Lab (Virtualization):

Before you start experimenting, you need a safe environment. Messing around with live systems without permission is a recipe for disaster. That's why we'll be using virtualization.

Virtualization allows you to run one operating system inside another. This means you can create isolated virtual machines (VMs) where you can test your hacking skills without affecting your main system. I recommend using VirtualBox or VMware Player, both of which are free and easy to set up.

[Personal Insight Placeholder 1: I remember the first time I tried exploiting a vulnerability on a live network... it didn't end well! Setting up a lab environment is the single most important thing you can do to protect yourself and others.]

Book Overview & Learning Objectives:

This book is designed to give you a solid foundation in Linux and its application to ethical hacking. By the end of this book, you'll be able to:

- Confidently navigate the Linux command line.
- Understand basic networking concepts.
- Use essential security tools like Nmap and Wireshark.
- Write simple Bash scripts to automate tasks.
- Identify and exploit basic vulnerabilities (in a controlled environment, of course!).
- Apply security best practices to protect your systems.

We'll be using Kali Linux, a distribution specifically designed for penetration testing. It comes pre-loaded with hundreds of security tools, making it an ideal platform for learning.

This is just the beginning of your journey. Cybersecurity is a constantly evolving field, and there's always something new to learn. But with a solid foundation in

Linux and ethical hacking principles, you'll be well-equipped to tackle the challenges ahead. Let's get started!

Next Steps:
The next chapter will be diving deeper into Linux foundations. Stay tuned.

Chapter 1: Linux Foundations

Welcome to the heart of the hacking world! Before we dive into fancy tools and exciting exploits, we need to build a solid foundation. This chapter will cover the essential Linux concepts you need to understand before moving forward. Think of it as laying the groundwork for a skyscraper – you can't build anything impressive without a strong base.

1.1 What is Linux? (History, Open Source)

So, Linux. You hear about it all the time, especially in the context of hacking and cybersecurity. But what *actually* is it? Is it just some nerdy operating system for bearded programmers? Well, partly, yes! But it's also much, much more. It's a philosophy, a community, and a powerhouse of innovation. To really grasp what Linux is, we need to take a quick trip back in time.

A Spark of Inspiration: The Early Days

Our story begins in the early 1990s, with a young Finnish computer science student named Linus Torvalds. He was using MINIX, a simplified Unix-like operating system, but he felt limited by its constraints. He wanted something more powerful, more customizable, and…well, more free.

Linus started working on his own operating system kernel – the core of the OS that manages the hardware and interacts with applications. He shared his work online, and soon other programmers started contributing. This collaborative effort was crucial.

Enter the Kernel: The Heart of Linux

The heart of the Linux operating system is its *kernel*. The kernel is the core program that manages the computer's resources, including the CPU, memory, and input/output devices. It's the bridge between the hardware and the software.

Linus Torvalds continues to maintain the Linux kernel to this day. It's an impressive feat considering the sheer size and complexity of the project. The kernel is constantly being updated, improved, and patched by a global community of developers.

[Personal Insight Placeholder: I remember reading about Linus Torvalds back in the day and being amazed that one person could create something so impactful. It really highlighted the power of individual initiative and open collaboration.]

The Power of Open Source: More Than Just "Free"

But Linux is more than just a kernel. What truly sets it apart is its open-source nature. This means the source code – the human-readable instructions that make up the OS – is freely available to anyone.

The implications of this are enormous:

- **Transparency:** Anyone can inspect the code, find bugs, and verify that there are no hidden backdoors or malicious code. This level of transparency is unheard of in proprietary operating systems.
- **Customization:** You're not stuck with the way the OS is designed. You can modify it to fit your specific needs. This is particularly valuable for hackers who need a system that can be tailored to their tasks.
- **Collaboration:** Open source fosters collaboration. Developers from all over the world contribute to Linux, constantly improving it and fixing vulnerabilities. This collective intelligence makes Linux incredibly robust and secure.
- **Freedom:** You're free to use Linux for any purpose, commercial or non-commercial, without paying licensing fees. This makes it accessible to everyone, regardless of their budget.

It's important to understand that "open source" doesn't just mean "free of charge" (although it often is). It's about the *freedom* to use, study, modify, and distribute the software. This freedom is what empowers users and drives innovation.

From Kernel to Distribution: Choosing Your Flavor of Linux

While the kernel is essential, it's not a complete operating system by itself. You need other components, such as system utilities, a desktop environment (like GNOME or KDE), and applications. This is where Linux *distributions* (or "distros") come in.

A Linux distribution is a complete operating system built around the Linux kernel. There are hundreds of different distributions, each tailored to specific needs and preferences.

- **Ubuntu:** A popular choice for beginners due to its ease of use and large community support.

- **Fedora:** A community-driven distribution known for its cutting-edge technology.
- **Debian:** A stable and reliable distribution often used for servers.
- **Kali Linux:** And, of course, our focus in this book! A distribution specifically designed for penetration testing and digital forensics, pre-loaded with a vast array of security tools.

The sheer number of distributions might seem overwhelming, but it's a testament to the flexibility of Linux. You can choose a distro that perfectly fits your requirements.

[Personal Insight Placeholder: When I was first starting out, I distro-hopped like crazy! I tried everything from Arch Linux (which requires you to build the system from scratch) to Gentoo (which compiles everything from source code). It was a great learning experience, but I eventually settled on Debian-based systems for their stability and ease of use.]

In Summary:

Linux is much more than just an operating system. It's a powerful combination of:

- A robust and efficient kernel.
- A vibrant open-source community.
- A philosophy of transparency, collaboration, and freedom.

Understanding these core concepts is crucial for anyone serious about hacking and cybersecurity. In the following sections, we'll dive deeper into Kali Linux and explore how it can be used to defend systems.

Is there anything specific you'd like me to elaborate on in this section? Perhaps a comparison to other operating systems, or a more detailed explanation of a specific concept?

1.2 Understanding the Linux Kernel and Distributions: Separating the Core from the Package

We've established that Linux is an operating system. But, unlike Windows or macOS where the entire OS is a single, tightly controlled entity, Linux has a slightly more nuanced structure. This section breaks down the key players: the kernel and the distributions, or "distros," and explains how they work together. Think of it like understanding the relationship between an engine and a car.

The Linux Kernel: The Engine Under the Hood

At the very heart of any Linux-based system lies the *kernel.* Imagine it as the core engine of a car – without it, the whole thing just doesn't run. The kernel is the foundational software responsible for:

- **Hardware Management:** This includes managing the CPU, memory (RAM), storage devices (hard drives, SSDs), and peripherals (printers, keyboards, mice). It acts as the intermediary between software and hardware, allowing applications to access and utilize the computer's resources.
- **Process Management:** The kernel is responsible for creating, scheduling, and terminating processes (running programs). It ensures that each process gets the resources it needs to run efficiently without interfering with other processes.
- **File System Management:** The kernel provides a structured way to organize and access files on storage devices. It manages the file system hierarchy, permissions, and access control.
- **System Calls:** The kernel provides a set of system calls that allow applications to request services from the kernel, such as reading or writing files, creating new processes, or accessing network resources. These are the "official" ways for programs to interact with the OS core.

The Linux kernel is maintained primarily by Linus Torvalds and a team of dedicated developers. They constantly work to improve its performance, stability, and security. It's a continuously evolving project, adapting to new hardware and software technologies.

Distributions: The Complete Car, Ready to Drive

Now, the kernel alone is like a bare engine. You can't just put an engine on the road and expect to drive. You need a chassis, wheels, seats, a steering wheel, and all the other components that make up a complete car. In the Linux world, these "complete car" packages are called *distributions* or *distros*.

A Linux distribution takes the Linux kernel and adds a bunch of other software components to create a fully functional operating system. This includes things like:

- **System Utilities:** These are essential tools for managing the system, such as command-line utilities, file managers, and text editors.
- **Desktop Environment (GUI):** This provides a graphical user interface (GUI) for interacting with the system. Common desktop environments

include GNOME, KDE, XFCE, and LXDE. (Kali uses XFCE by default because it's lightweight).
- **Applications:** This includes a wide range of applications, such as web browsers, office suites, media players, and development tools.
- **Package Manager:** A tool for installing, updating, and removing software packages. Common package managers include apt (used in Debian-based distributions like Kali and Ubuntu), yum (used in Fedora and CentOS), and pacman (used in Arch Linux).

Why So Many Distros? The Beauty of Choice

You might be wondering why there are so many different Linux distributions. The answer lies in the open-source nature of Linux and the diverse needs of its users. Because anyone can modify and redistribute the kernel and other software components, different groups have created distributions tailored to specific purposes.

Here are some common reasons for creating new Linux distributions:

- **Specific Use Cases:** Some distributions are designed for specific tasks, such as server administration, embedded systems, or penetration testing (like Kali Linux).
- **User Experience:** Different distributions offer different desktop environments and user interfaces, catering to different preferences.
- **Philosophy:** Some distributions adhere to specific philosophical principles, such as a commitment to free software or a focus on stability and reliability.
- **Community:** Each distribution has its own community of developers and users, which can provide support and contribute to the development of the distribution.

Kali Linux: The Hacker's Choice

In our case, we're focusing on Kali Linux. It's purpose-built for cybersecurity professionals and ethical hackers. This means it comes pre-loaded with a comprehensive suite of tools for:

- **Information Gathering (Reconnaissance)**
- **Vulnerability Analysis**
- **Exploitation**
- **Forensics**
- **Reverse Engineering**

Instead of spending hours installing and configuring these tools yourself, they're all ready to go right out of the box in Kali. This makes it an efficient and effective platform for learning and practicing your hacking skills.

Kernel and Distribution: A Symbiotic Relationship

To summarize, the Linux kernel is the core engine, while the distribution is the complete car. The kernel provides the fundamental functionality, while the distribution provides the user-friendly interface, applications, and tools that make the system usable.

Understanding this relationship is crucial for anyone working with Linux. It allows you to appreciate the flexibility and power of the operating system and to choose the distribution that best suits your needs.

Next Steps
Next up, we will explore the purpose and philosophy of Kali Linux

1.3 Introduction to Kali Linux: Purpose & Philosophy: More Than Just a Collection of Tools

Okay, we've talked about Linux in general, and now it's time to zoom in on our star distribution: Kali Linux. You might think of Kali as just a collection of hacking tools bundled together. And while that's certainly *part* of it, there's a deeper purpose and philosophy driving this particular flavor of Linux.

Purpose: A Swiss Army Knife for Security Professionals

Kali Linux is specifically designed for penetration testing, security auditing, and digital forensics. It's the operating system of choice for ethical hackers, cybersecurity professionals, and anyone who needs a comprehensive toolkit for assessing and securing systems.

Here's a breakdown of the key areas where Kali excels:

- **Penetration Testing:** Kali provides a vast array of tools for simulating real-world attacks to identify vulnerabilities in systems and networks. This includes tools for reconnaissance, vulnerability scanning, exploitation, and post-exploitation.

- **Security Auditing:** Kali can be used to assess the security posture of organizations, identifying weaknesses in their policies, procedures, and infrastructure.
- **Digital Forensics:** Kali includes tools for investigating digital evidence, recovering deleted files, and analyzing network traffic. This is crucial for incident response and law enforcement investigations.
- **Reverse Engineering:** Kali has tools useful for taking software, malware, or system files and investigating how they operate by disassembling the executable code.

It's important to remember that Kali is a specialized distribution. It's not designed to be a general-purpose operating system for everyday use. While you *can* use it for browsing the web or writing documents, its primary focus is on security tasks.

Pre-Installed Tools: A Hacker's Dream

One of the biggest advantages of Kali Linux is that it comes pre-loaded with hundreds of security tools. These tools are categorized into different areas, making it easy to find what you need for a specific task.

Some of the most popular categories include:

- **Information Gathering:** Tools for gathering information about targets, such as Nmap, whois, and DNSenum.
- **Vulnerability Analysis:** Tools for scanning systems and networks for vulnerabilities, such as Nessus, OpenVAS, and Nikto.
- **Exploitation Tools:** Frameworks and tools for exploiting identified vulnerabilities, such as Metasploit, and exploit-db.
- **Wireless Attacks:** Tools for attacking wireless networks, such as Aircrack-ng and Reaver.
- **Web Applications:** Tools for testing the security of web applications, such as Burp Suite and OWASP ZAP.
- **Forensics Tools:** Tools for analyzing disk images, recovering deleted files, and investigating network traffic.

Philosophy: More Than Just a Toolkit

Beyond the impressive collection of tools, Kali Linux adheres to a specific philosophy:

- **Open Source:** Kali is completely open source, meaning its source code is freely available for anyone to inspect, modify, and redistribute. This transparency is crucial for security, as it allows anyone to verify that there are no hidden backdoors or malicious code.

- **Free as in Beer:** Kali Linux is free of charge for anyone to use, commercial or non-commercial. This makes it accessible to everyone, regardless of their budget.
- **Customization:** Kali is highly customizable. You can easily add or remove tools, tweak configurations, and optimize performance to suit your specific needs.
- **Adherence to Standards:** Kali adheres to open standards, ensuring compatibility with other systems and tools.
- **Community-Driven:** Kali is actively supported by a large and vibrant community of developers and users. This community provides support, contributes to the development of Kali, and helps to ensure its security and reliability.
- **Focus on Security:** Above all, Kali is designed with security in mind. It minimizes unnecessary services and potential attack surfaces, making it a secure platform for security tasks.

Who Should Use Kali Linux?

Kali Linux is primarily intended for:

- **Ethical Hackers and Penetration Testers:** Those who are legally authorized to assess the security of systems and networks.
- **Security Auditors:** Professionals who evaluate the security posture of organizations.
- **Digital Forensics Investigators:** Those who investigate digital evidence in criminal or civil cases.
- **Security Researchers:** Those who study vulnerabilities and develop security tools.

It's *not* recommended for beginners who are just starting to learn about Linux or cybersecurity. Kali requires a certain level of technical expertise and a solid understanding of security principles. However, since this book takes you from basics up, that initial hurdle is reduced.

Responsible Use is Key

It's crucial to remember that the tools in Kali Linux can be used for both good and evil. It's your responsibility to use them ethically and legally. Unauthorized access to computer systems is illegal and can have serious consequences.

This book will focus on the *ethical* use of Kali Linux for penetration testing and security auditing. We will emphasize the importance of obtaining proper authorization before testing any systems or networks.

In Summary:

Kali Linux is a powerful and versatile operating system that provides a comprehensive toolkit for security professionals. Its purpose is to enable ethical hacking, security auditing, and digital forensics. Its philosophy is based on open source principles, customization, and a strong focus on security. But, it is just a tool and can be used for unethical and illegal practices. You must commit to using these skills ethically.

Now we can delve deeper into exploring the Kali desktop environment.

1.4 Navigating the Kali Desktop Environment: Getting Around Like a Pro

Alright, you've got Kali installed (or you're about to!), and it's time to get familiar with your surroundings. Think of the desktop environment as the cockpit of a spaceship. You need to know where the controls are, what the instruments mean, and how to navigate efficiently if you're going to pilot it successfully.

XFCE: Lightweight and Customizable

By default, Kali Linux uses the XFCE desktop environment. XFCE is known for being lightweight, fast, and highly customizable. This makes it a great choice for penetration testing, where performance and flexibility are crucial. XFCE is chosen as the default because of its low impact on system resources, allowing for better performance in resource-intensive tasks. It is also easily customizable for the needs of advanced users.

Don't expect a flashy, resource-intensive experience. XFCE prioritizes function over form. However, you can customize its appearance to your liking.

Key Components of the Kali Desktop

Let's break down the main components of the Kali desktop:

- **The Desktop:** This is the main area where you'll see your icons, windows, and applications. You can right-click on the desktop to access a menu with options for creating new files and folders, changing the background, and opening a terminal.

- **The Panel (Taskbar):** Typically located at the top or bottom of the screen (usually top by default), the panel provides quick access to essential features:
    - **Applications Menu:** This is where you'll find all the applications installed on Kali, organized into categories. It's like the Start Menu in Windows.
    - **Launcher Icons:** These are shortcuts to frequently used applications, such as the terminal, web browser, and file manager.
    - **System Tray:** This area displays information about system status, such as network connectivity, battery level, and volume control.
    - **Workspace Switcher:** XFCE supports multiple workspaces, allowing you to organize your applications into different virtual desktops. This can be helpful for managing multiple tasks or projects.
- **The Terminal:** This is your command-line interface, and it's where you'll be spending most of your time as a hacker. You can open a terminal by clicking the terminal icon in the panel or by searching for "terminal" in the applications menu.
- **The File Manager (Thunar):** Thunar is the default file manager in XFCE. It allows you to browse the file system, create new files and folders, copy and paste files, and perform other file management tasks.

Finding Your Way Around

The most important skill for navigating the Kali desktop is knowing how to find the tools you need. There are several ways to do this:

- **The Applications Menu:** Browse the categories in the applications menu to find tools related to a specific task.
- **The Search Bar:** Type the name of a tool or keyword into the search bar to quickly locate it.
- **The Command Line:** If you know the name of the command you want to run, you can simply type it into the terminal.

Customizing Your Environment

One of the great things about XFCE is that it's highly customizable. You can change the appearance, add or remove panel items, and configure keyboard shortcuts to your liking.

Here are a few common customizations:

- **Changing the Theme:** You can change the overall look and feel of the desktop by selecting a different theme. Go to "Settings" -> "Appearance" to choose a theme.
- **Adding Panel Items:** You can add new items to the panel, such as launchers for frequently used applications or system monitors. Right-click on the panel and select "Panel" -> "Add New Items."
- **Configuring Keyboard Shortcuts:** You can assign keyboard shortcuts to frequently used commands or applications. Go to "Settings" -> "Keyboard" -> "Application Shortcuts."
- **Using Different Icons**: Customize the appearance of your desktop

Essential Kali Applications to Know

While Kali comes with a TON of applications pre-installed, here are a few you should get familiar with early on:

- **Terminal:** (xfce4-terminal) Your primary interface.
- **Burp Suite:** (Professional version requires a license) Web application security testing framework.
- **Wireshark:** Network packet analyzer.
- **Nmap:** Network scanner.
- **Metasploit Framework:** Exploitation framework (command line: msfconsole).
- **Thunar:** (File Manager)

Hands-On Exploration

The best way to learn the Kali desktop environment is to explore it yourself. Take some time to click around, experiment with different settings, and try out different applications. Don't be afraid to break things – you can always reinstall Kali if you mess something up!

- Try changing the desktop background.
- Add a new launcher to the panel.
- Create a new workspace and move an application to it.
- Open the terminal and run a few basic commands (like ls, cd, and pwd).

Remember, the goal is to become comfortable with your environment so that you can focus on the task at hand.

In Summary:

The Kali Linux desktop environment, powered by XFCE, is a flexible and efficient platform for ethical hacking and cybersecurity tasks. By understanding the key components and customizing it to your liking, you can create a workspace that empowers you to be more productive and effective. So, fire up Kali, explore, and get comfortable!

We'll be diving into command-line operations in the next section. This is where things start getting *really* interesting.

1.5 Basic Command Line Operations: ls, cd, pwd, mkdir, rm: Your First Steps to Command-Line Mastery

Welcome to the world of the command line! If you're new to Linux (or even if you're not), the command line might seem intimidating. But trust me, mastering the basics is one of the most important things you can do as a hacker. Think of it as learning the alphabet before writing a novel. These basic commands are the building blocks for everything else you'll do.

Why the Command Line Matters

Why bother with typing commands when you can just click around in a graphical interface? Because the command line offers power, flexibility, and automation that simply aren't possible with a GUI. Here's why it's essential for hackers:

- **Precise Control:** The command line allows you to interact with the system at a very granular level, giving you precise control over every aspect of your environment.
- **Automation:** You can automate repetitive tasks by writing scripts that execute a series of commands. This can save you a lot of time and effort.
- **Remote Access:** The command line is the primary way to interact with remote servers and systems.
- **Tool Interaction:** Many security tools are designed to be used primarily from the command line.
- **Efficiency:** Once you become proficient, the command line can be much faster and more efficient than using a GUI.

Opening a Terminal

Before we start, you need to open a terminal. Click the terminal icon in the panel or search for "terminal" in the applications menu. You'll see a prompt that looks something like kali@kali:~$. This indicates your current username (kali), the hostname of the system (kali), and your current directory (~, which is your home directory). Don't worry if it looks different on your system.

Essential Commands: The Core Five

Let's learn the five most basic commands that every Linux user should know: ls, cd, pwd, mkdir, and rm. These commands allow you to list files, change directories, print your current directory, create new directories, and remove files and directories.

- **ls (list): Listing Files and Folders**

  The ls command lists the files and directories in the current directory. It's the most basic way to see what's around you.

  ```
  ls
  ```

  This will show you a simple list of the files and directories in your current location. But ls has several useful options:

  - **ls -l (long listing):** Displays a detailed listing with permissions, ownership, size, modification date, and more. This is incredibly useful for understanding file attributes.

    ```
    ls -l
    ```

  - **ls -a (all):** Shows hidden files and directories (those starting with a .). These files often contain configuration settings.

    ```
    ls -a
    ```

  - **ls -h (human-readable):** Displays file sizes in a more human-readable format (e.g., 1K, 234M, 2G) instead of bytes. This works best in conjunction with -l.

    ```
    ls -lh
    ```

- **cd (change directory): Moving Around**

The cd command changes your current directory. This is how you navigate the file system.

- **cd directory_name:** Changes to the specified directory.

```
cd Documents
```

- **cd ..:** Moves you up one directory level (to the parent directory).

```
cd ..
```

- **cd:** Takes you back to your home directory. This is a quick way to get back to familiar territory.

```
cd
```

- **cd -:** Returns you to the previous directory you were in

```
cd -
```

- **pwd (print working directory): Where Am I?**

  The pwd command displays your current directory. This is useful if you get lost or confused about where you are in the file system.

```
pwd
```

- **mkdir (make directory): Creating New Spaces**

  The mkdir command creates a new directory. This is how you organize your files and projects.

```
mkdir my_new_directory
```

- **rm (remove): Deleting Files (Use with Caution!)**

The rm command deletes files and directories. **This is a powerful command, and you should use it with extreme caution.** There's no "undo" button!

- **rm filename:** Deletes the specified file.

  ```
  rm myfile.txt
  ```

- **rm -r directory_name:** Deletes the specified directory and all its contents (recursively). This is especially dangerous!

  ```
  rm -r my_important_directory
  ```

- **rm -i filename:** Prompts you to confirm before deleting each file. Use this with extreme caution.

[Personal Insight Placeholder 1: I've accidentally wiped out entire projects with a misplaced rm -rf. It's a humbling experience that taught me the importance of double-checking my commands before pressing Enter.]

Tab Completion: Your Best Friend

The command line can be tedious, but there's a trick that can save you a lot of typing: tab completion. Just start typing a file or directory name and press the Tab key. The shell will try to complete the name for you. If there are multiple possibilities, it will show you a list.

Example: If you have a directory called "MyHackingProject," you can type cd MyHac and then press Tab. The shell will automatically complete the name to cd MyHackingProject.

Hands-On Practice: Experiment!

The best way to learn these commands is to practice. Try the following exercises:

1. Create a new directory called "test_area".
2. Change into the "test_area" directory.
3. Create three new files: "file1.txt", "file2.txt", and "file3.txt". (You can use the touch command to create empty files: touch file1.txt)
4. List the files in the "test_area" directory.

5. Delete "file2.txt".
6. Go back to your home directory.
7. Remove the "test_area" directory (and all its contents).

In Summary:

These five commands – ls, cd, pwd, mkdir, and rm – are the foundation of your command-line skills. Mastering them will give you a solid base for exploring the rest of the Linux world. Practice them regularly, and you'll be surprised how quickly they become second nature.

Chapter 2: Mastering the Command Line: Beyond the Basics

Congratulations! You've taken your first steps into the command-line world. Now it's time to level up! This chapter will build upon the foundation you established in Chapter 1 and teach you more advanced command-line skills. Think of it as learning to drive a car after mastering the basics of steering and braking. We will delve deeper into the command line interface, explore file manipulation and navigation, understand how redirection and piping help, see how file permissions work, and use package management using APT.

2.1 File System Navigation & Manipulation: Becoming a File System Ninja

You've taken the first step by understanding the basic commands for moving around the Linux file system. Now, it's time to sharpen those skills and become a true File System Ninja! This isn't just about getting from point A to point B; it's about mastering the art of finding, creating, and organizing files with speed and precision.

Understanding Paths: The GPS of Your File System

Before we dive into fancy techniques, let's solidify our understanding of paths – the addresses that guide us through the file system. There are two main types of paths: absolute and relative.

- **Absolute Paths: Starting from the Top**

An absolute path is like giving someone the precise GPS coordinates to a location. It starts from the root directory (/) and specifies the *entire* route to the file or directory you want to access.

For example, /home/kali/Documents/my_report.txt is an absolute path. It tells you exactly where my_report.txt is located, starting from the top of the file system.

Using absolute paths ensures that you always reach the correct destination, regardless of your current location. However, they can be long and tedious to type.

- **Relative Paths: Navigating from Where You Are**

  A relative path, on the other hand, is like giving someone directions from their current location. It specifies the route to the file or directory relative to your *current working directory*.

  For example, if you're currently in /home/kali, the relative path to my_report.txt would be Documents/my_report.txt. It's shorter and easier to type.

  The key to using relative paths effectively is understanding your current working directory. You can always use the pwd command to display your current directory.

Special Directory Shortcuts: Mastering the Symbols

Linux provides some handy shortcuts for commonly used directories:

- . (dot): Represents the current directory.

  This might not seem useful at first, but it comes in handy when you need to specify the current directory in a command. For example, to execute a script in the current directory, you can use ./my_script.sh.

  ```
  ./my_script.sh
  ```

- .. (dot dot): Represents the parent directory.

This is your go-to shortcut for moving up one level in the file system. It's much easier than typing out the full path to the parent directory.

```
cd ..
```

- ~ (tilde): Represents your home directory.

  This is a quick and easy way to return to your home directory, no matter where you are in the file system.

  ```
  cd ~
  ```

Practical Examples: Putting It All Together

Let's put these concepts into practice with some examples:

1. **Create a directory structure:**

   ```
   mkdir -p my_project/src/include
   cd my_project/src
   pwd
   ```

   This command creates the my_project directory, the src directory inside my_project, and the include directory inside src. The -p option tells mkdir to create parent directories as needed.

2. Now navigate to the include directory using relative paths:

   ```
   cd ../include
   pwd
   ```

3. Now navigate to the include directory using absolute paths:

   ```
   cd /home/kali/my_project/src/include
   pwd
   ```

   Now make the parent directories private to you (700) and the final include directory readable to other users

```
chmod 700 /home/kali/my_project
chmod 700 /home/kali/my_project/src
chmod 744 /home/kali/my_project/src/include
```

Listing Files with Wildcards: The Power of Patterns

Wildcards are special characters that allow you to match multiple files or directories based on a pattern. This can save you a lot of typing and make it easier to find the files you need.

- * (asterisk): Matches any character or sequence of characters (except for a leading dot in filenames).

  For example, ls *.txt lists all files ending in .txt in the current directory.

  ```
  touch file1.txt file2.txt file3.log
  ls *.txt
  ```

- ? (question mark): Matches any single character.

  For example, ls file?.txt lists files like "file1.txt" and "fileA.txt".

  ```
  touch file1.txt fileA.txt file22.txt
  ls file?.txt
  ```

- [] (square brackets): Matches any character within the brackets.

  For example, ls file[1-3].txt lists "file1.txt", "file2.txt", and "file3.txt".

  ```
  touch file1.txt file2.txt file3.txt file4.txt
  ls file[1-3].txt
  ```

- [!...] (square brackets with exclamation mark): Matches any character *not* within the brackets.

  For example, ls file[!1-3].txt lists files that are *not* "file1.txt", "file2.txt", and "file3.txt".

  ```
  touch file1.txt file2.txt file3.txt file4.txt
  ls file[!1-3].txt
  ```

Practical Examples: Using Wildcards Like a Pro

1. **Find all configuration files:**

   ```
   ls /etc/*config*
   ```

   This command lists all files in the /etc directory that have "config" in their name.

2. **List all files starting with "report" and ending in ".pdf":**

   ```
   ls report*.pdf
   ```

3. **List all files starting with "data" followed by a single digit and ending in ".csv":**

   ```
   ls data?.csv
   ```

4. **List all files starting with "image" followed by a number between 0 and 9 followed by either .jpg or .png":**

   ```
   ls image[0-9].[jpg|png]
   ```

Code Documentation Style:

- **Comments:** Add comments to your code to explain what it does and why.
- **Variable Names:** Use meaningful variable names to improve readability.
- **Indentation:** Use consistent indentation to make your code easier to follow.

[Personal Insight Placeholder 2: When I'm working on a complex project, I use wildcards and tab completion constantly. It's the only way to keep track of all the files and directories.]

Next Steps

Practice. Experiment. Get comfortable with these commands and techniques. The more you use them, the more natural they will become. This is just the beginning. You can also learn about more advanced features like using regular expressions with find and grep.

What shall we work on next?

2.2 Working with Files: cat, less, head, tail, grep, find: Unveiling the Secrets Within

You're becoming a file system ninja, but knowing *how* to navigate is only half the battle. You also need to know *how* to extract useful information from files. This section introduces you to essential commands for reading, searching, and finding files: cat, less, head, tail, grep, and find. These are your tools for uncovering the secrets hidden within.

cat (concatenate): A Quick Peek

The cat command is the simplest way to display the entire contents of a file to the terminal. It's like taking a quick peek inside.

```
cat my_file.txt
```

This command will print the entire contents of my_file.txt to your terminal. It's useful for small files but can be overwhelming for larger files.

Example:

Let's say you have a file named greeting.txt with the following content:

```
      Hello, world!
This is a simple greeting.
```

Running cat greeting.txt would display:

```
      Hello, world!
This is a simple greeting.
```

[Personal Insight Placeholder 1: I often use cat to quickly view configuration files or small scripts. It's a fast and easy way to see what's inside.]

less (less is more): The Gentle Reader

The less command is a more sophisticated way to view files. It allows you to page through the file, one screen at a time. This is ideal for viewing large files.

```
less my_large_file.txt
```

- **Navigation:**
  - Use the arrow keys to scroll up and down.
  - Press the Spacebar to move to the next page.
  - Press b to move to the previous page.
  - Press g to go to the beginning of the file.
  - Press G to go to the end of the file.
- **Searching:**
  - Type /search_term and press Enter to search for a specific term.
  - Press n to go to the next match.
  - Press N to go to the previous match.
- **Exiting:**
  - Press q to quit less.

Example:

Open a long configuration file (like /etc/ssh/sshd_config) with less and try navigating and searching for different options.

```
less /etc/ssh/sshd_config
```

head and tail: The Beginning and the End

The head command displays the first few lines of a file, while the tail command displays the last few lines. These are invaluable for examining log files to see the most recent entries.

- **head:** Displays the first 10 lines by default.

  ```
  head my_file.txt
  ```

  Use the -n option to specify the number of lines to display.

```
head -n 20 my_file.txt  # Displays the first 20 lines
```

- **tail:** Displays the last 10 lines by default.

  ```
  tail my_file.txt
  ```

  Use the -n option to specify the number of lines to display.

  ```
  tail -n 5 my_file.txt  # Displays the last 5 lines
  ```

  The tail -f command is particularly useful for monitoring log files in real time. It will display new lines as they are added to the file.

  ```
  tail -f /var/log/syslog  # Monitor the system log
  ```

Example:

Monitor the Apache access log to see new requests as they come in.
Please make sure your web server is properly configured to allow you to see these log files.

```
sudo tail -f /var/log/apache2/access.log
```

[Personal Insight Placeholder 2: I often use tail -f to debug web applications. I can see the requests coming in and the errors being logged in real time.]

grep (global regular expression print): The Pattern Hunter

The grep command searches for lines in a file that match a specific pattern. It's one of the most powerful tools for analyzing text files.

```
grep "error" /var/log/syslog  # Find all lines containing "error"
```

grep Options

- -i: Case-insensitive search.

```
grep -i "error" /var/log/syslog
```

- -v: Invert the search (show lines that *don't* match the pattern).

```
grep -v "error" /var/log/syslog  # Show lines that don't
contain "error"
```

- -n: Print the line numbers of matching lines.

```
grep -n "error" /var/log/syslog
```

- -r: Recursive search (search within directories).

```
grep -r "password" /etc/  # Search for "password" in all
files under /etc/
```

Example:

Search for all lines in the Apache configuration files that contain the word "Directory".

Please ensure that you have enough permissions to list these files.

```
grep -r "Directory" /etc/apache2/
```

find: The Master Locator

The find command searches for files and directories that match specific criteria. It can search the entire file system or just a specific directory.

```
find / -name "myfile.txt"  # Find a file named "myfile.txt" in the
entire system
```

Practical Examples

1. Find all files modified in the last 24 hours

```
find . -mtime -1
```

2. Find all files that do *not* end in ".txt"

```
find . ! -name "*.txt"
```

3. Change the permissions for all files that end in .sh to be executable

   ```
   find . -name "*.sh" -exec chmod +x {} \;
   ```

   This command combines find with -exec. -exec executes a command for each file found, and the {} is a placeholder for the filename. The \; is needed to tell find where the command ends.

4. Find all .txt files that contain the word "password".

   ```
   find . -name "*.txt" -exec grep -l "password" {} \;
   ```

   Explanation:

   - find . -name "*.txt": Finds all files with the .txt extension in the current directory and its subdirectories.
   - -exec grep -l "password" {} \;: Executes the grep -l "password" {} command on each file found.
     - -exec command {} \;: Executes the specified command on each file found by find.
     - grep -l "password" {}: Searches for the string "password" within the current file (represented by {}). The -l option makes grep only output the filenames containing the string, rather than the matching lines themselves.
5. Remove all files ending in .tmp in the current directory:

   ```
   find . -name "*.tmp" -exec rm {} \;
   ```

Documentation Style:

- **Comments:** Add comments to your code to explain what it does and why.
- **Variable Names:** Use meaningful variable names to improve readability.
- **Indentation:** Use consistent indentation to make your code easier to follow.

Putting It All Together: A Practical Scenario

Imagine you're investigating a security incident on a web server. You want to find all the log entries related to a specific IP address (e.g., 192.168.1.100) that occurred in the last 24 hours.

Here's how you could do it using the commands you've learned:

1. Find all log files modified in the last 24 hours (assuming your logs are in /var/log/apache2/).

```
find /var/log/apache2/ -mtime -1
```

2. Grep the specific IP address in the logs.

```
grep "192.168.1.100" <log file>
```

These examples are a start. The more you practice, the better you'll become at choosing the right tool for the job and combining commands to solve complex problems.

What do you think? Ready to move on, or should we refine this section further?

2.3 Redirection & Piping: Combining Commands for Maximum Power: Unleash the Command-Line Symphony

You've learned how to use individual commands to perform specific tasks. Now, it's time to learn how to combine commands to create powerful workflows. Redirection and piping are the secret ingredients that allow you to unleash the full potential of the command line. Think of it like learning to orchestrate different instruments to create a symphony.

Redirection: Channeling the Flow

Redirection allows you to change the standard input, standard output, or standard error streams of a command. This means you can redirect the output of a command to a file, use the contents of a file as the input for a command, or capture error messages for analysis.

- > (Output Redirection): Saving the Results

  The > operator redirects the standard output of a command to a file. If the file already exists, it will be overwritten.

  ```
  ls -l > file_list.txt
  ```

This command saves the output of ls -l (a detailed listing of files and directories) to a file named file_list.txt. The original contents of file_list.txt will be lost (if there was an earlier version).

Practical Example:

1. Create a directory named redirection_test.
2. Change into the redirection_test directory.
3. Run ls -l > file_list.txt.
4. Verify that a file named file_list.txt has been created and that it contains the output of the ls -l command.

```
mkdir redirection_test
cd redirection_test
ls -l > file_list.txt
cat file_list.txt
```

- >> (Append Redirection): Adding to the Story

The >> operator redirects the standard output of a command to a file, appending it to the end of the file if it already exists. This is useful for adding data to a log file or creating a cumulative report.

```
date >> log_file.txt
```

This command appends the current date and time to the log_file.txt file.

Practical Example:

1. Create a file named my_log.txt.
2. Run echo "Starting process..." >> my_log.txt.
3. Run date >> my_log.txt.
4. Verify that the my_log.txt file contains both the "Starting process..." message and the current date and time.

```
touch my_log.txt
echo "Starting process..." >> my_log.txt
date >> my_log.txt
cat my_log.txt
```

- < (Input Redirection): Feeding the Machine

The < operator redirects the standard input of a command from a file. This is less common than output redirection, but it's useful for commands that read input from standard input.

```
wc -l < file_list.txt
```

This command counts the number of lines in file_list.txt using the wc -l command, which normally reads input from the keyboard.

Practical Example:

1. Create a file named word_list.txt with a list of words, one word per line.
2. Run sort < word_list.txt.
3. Verify that the words are sorted alphabetically (the output will be displayed in the terminal).

```
echo -e "zebra\napple\nbanana" > word_list.txt
      sort < word_list.txt
```

Piping: The Assembly Line

Piping is where the real magic happens. The | (pipe) operator takes the standard output of one command and uses it as the standard input for another command. This allows you to create complex chains of commands that perform sophisticated tasks. Think of it as an assembly line, where each command performs a specific step in the process.

```
ls -l | grep "txt"
```

This command lists files and directories with ls -l and then filters the output to show only the lines that contain "txt" using grep.

Practical Examples:

1. **Find all running processes owned by a specific user:**

```
ps aux | grep username
```

- ps aux: Lists all running processes on the system.
- grep username: Filters the output to show only the processes owned by "username".
  Please change "username" with the correct account name.

2. **Count the number of files in a directory:**

```
ls -l | grep "^-" | wc -l
```

- ls -l: Lists the files and directories in the current directory.
- grep "^-": Filters the output to show only regular files (lines starting with "-").
- wc -l: Counts the number of lines in the filtered output.

3. **Find the largest files in a directory (using du, sort, and head):**

```
du -ah . | sort -rh | head -n 10
```

- du -ah .: Calculates the disk usage of each file and directory in the current directory (.).
- sort -rh: Sorts the output in reverse order (largest to smallest) and uses human-readable units (e.g., KB, MB, GB).
- head -n 10: Displays the top 10 largest files and directories.
  Note that without -h, you'll be sorting the output in bytes instead.

4. **Extract a specific column from a CSV file (using cut):**

```
cut -d "," -f 2 data.csv
```

- cut: A command for cutting out sections of a line by field
- -d ",": Specifies the delimiter as a comma (,).
- -f 2: Selects the second field (column).
- data.csv: Specifies the input file.

This command extracts the second column from a CSV file named data.csv. (The first column would be the index 1).

5. **Converting a file from lowercase to uppercase:**

```
tr [:lower:] [:upper:] < input.txt > output.txt
```

This command uses tr to convert all lowercase characters in input.txt to uppercase, and then saves the result to output.txt. tr is a tool used to translate or delete characters.

Practical Scenario: Analyzing Web Server Logs

Let's revisit the web server log analysis scenario from the previous section. You want to find all the log entries related to a specific IP address (e.g., 192.168.1.100) that occurred on a specific date (e.g., 2024-01-01).

Here's how you could do it using redirection and piping:

1. Grep the IP address and then the date (combining two steps into one):

   ```
   grep "192.168.1.100" access.log | grep "2024-01-01"
   ```

2. Sort the logs and save the result to a file:

```
grep "192.168.1.100" access.log | sort > ip_access.log
```

This demonstrates the power of combining commands using redirection and piping. With just a few simple commands, you can perform complex analysis tasks.

2.4 User Accounts & Permissions: Securing Your System

Understanding user accounts and permissions is crucial for securing your Linux system. Permissions control who can access and modify files and directories.

- **User Accounts:** Each user on a Linux system has a unique username and user ID (UID). The whoami command displays your current username. The /etc/passwd file contains information about all user accounts on the system.
- **Groups:** Users can be members of one or more groups. Groups allow you to grant permissions to multiple users at once. The groups command displays the groups that you are a member of. The /etc/group file contains information about all groups on the system.
- **File Permissions:** Each file and directory has three sets of permissions:
    - **Read (r):** Allows you to view the contents of a file or list the contents of a directory.
    - **Write (w):** Allows you to modify the contents of a file or create new files in a directory.

- **Execute (x):** Allows you to execute a file as a program or enter a directory.

These permissions are assigned to three categories of users:

- **Owner (u):** The user who owns the file or directory.
- **Group (g):** The group that owns the file or directory.
- **Other (o):** All other users on the system.

You can view the permissions of a file or directory using ls -l. The output will look something like this:

```
-rw-r--r-- 1 kali kali 1024 Jan 1 12:00 myfile.txt
drwxr-xr-x 2 kali kali 4096 Jan 1 12:00 mydirectory
```

The first character indicates the file type (- for regular file, d for directory). The next nine characters represent the permissions for the owner, group, and other users, respectively.

For example, -rw-r--r-- means:

- The owner has read and write permissions (rw-).
- The group has read permission (r--).
- Other users have read permission (r--).

- **chmod (change mode): Changing Permissions**

  The chmod command changes the permissions of a file or directory. You can use either numeric or symbolic notation to specify the new permissions.

  - **Numeric Notation:** Uses octal numbers to represent the permissions. Each number represents a combination of read, write, and execute permissions.
    - 4 = Read (r)
    - 2 = Write (w)
    - 1 = Execute (x)
    - 0 = No permission (-)

    To combine permissions, add the numbers together. For example, 6 (4+2) represents read and write permissions. 7 (4+2+1) represents read, write, and execute permissions.

To change the permissions of a file to read/write for the owner, read-only for the group, and read-only for others:

```
chmod 644 myfile.txt
```

- **Symbolic Notation:** Uses letters to represent the permissions.
    - u = Owner
    - g = Group
    - o = Other
    - a = All
    - + = Add permission
    - - = Remove permission
    - = = Set permission

To change the permissions of a file to read/write for the owner, read-only for the group, and read-only for others:

```
chmod u=rw,g=r,o=r myfile.txt
chmod u+w,g-w,o-w myfile.txt
```

- **chown (change owner): Changing Ownership**

The chown command changes the owner and/or group of a file or directory. You must be root or the current owner of the file to use chown.

```
sudo chown new_owner myfile.txt   # Change the owner to
new_owner
sudo chown :new_group myfile.txt   # Change the group to
new_group
sudo chown new_owner:new_group myfile.txt # Change both owner
and group
```

- **sudo (superuser do): Running Commands as Root**

The sudo command allows you to run commands as the root user (also known as the superuser). Root has unrestricted access to the system, so you should use sudo with caution.

```
sudo apt update   # Update the package lists
```

You will be prompted for your password when you use sudo.

2.5 Package Management (apt): Installing, Updating, and Removing Software: Your Gateway to the Software Universe

Imagine your operating system as a city. Package management is the system that allows you to easily install new buildings (software), upgrade existing ones, and demolish those you no longer need. In Kali Linux, this system is called apt (Advanced Package Tool). Mastering apt is essential for keeping your system up-to-date and installing the tools you need for penetration testing and other security tasks.

What is a Package?

Before we dive into the commands, let's understand what a "package" actually is. A package is a compressed archive containing all the files needed to install a specific piece of software. This includes:

- Executable files
- Configuration files
- Libraries
- Documentation

Packages also contain metadata (information about the software), such as the name, version, dependencies (other packages required by the software), and a description.

APT: The Package Manager Extraordinaire

apt is a powerful command-line tool that simplifies the process of managing packages. It automates tasks such as:

- Downloading packages from online repositories
- Resolving dependencies
- Installing files in the correct locations
- Configuring the software

Key apt Commands: Your Software Management Arsenal

Let's explore the most important apt commands:

- **apt update: Refreshing the Software List**

The apt update command updates the package lists from the software repositories. This means it downloads the latest information about available packages, including their names, versions, and dependencies. Think of it as updating the inventory list in a store. You should run apt update regularly to ensure that you have the most current information.

```
sudo apt update
```

Why sudo? You need root privileges to modify the system's package lists, so you must use sudo to run this command.

Practical Example:

1. Open a terminal.
2. Run sudo apt update.
3. Observe the output, which shows the progress of downloading package lists from various repositories.

```
sudo apt update
```

- **apt upgrade: Bringing Everything Up to Date**

  The apt upgrade command upgrades all installed packages to the latest versions available in the repositories. This helps to improve security, fix bugs, and add new features. Think of it as upgrading all the buildings in your city to the latest building codes. You should run apt upgrade regularly to keep your system secure and up-to-date.

```
sudo apt upgrade
```

Important: Before running apt upgrade, it's a good idea to run apt update to ensure that you have the latest package lists.

Practical Example:

1. Run sudo apt update.
2. Run sudo apt upgrade.
3. Observe the output, which shows the progress of upgrading packages.
4. You may be prompted to confirm the upgrade process.

```
sudo apt update
sudo apt upgrade
```

- **apt install: Adding New Tools to Your Arsenal**

  The apt install package_name command installs a new package. Replace package_name with the name of the package you want to install.

  ```
  sudo apt install wireshark
  ```

  This command installs the Wireshark network analyzer.

  Dependencies: apt will automatically resolve any dependencies required by the package you're installing. This means it will download and install any other packages that are needed for the software to function properly.

  Practical Example:

  1. Run sudo apt install nmap.
  2. Observe the output, which shows the progress of downloading and installing Nmap and its dependencies.
  3. After the installation is complete, run nmap -v to verify that Nmap is installed correctly.

  ```
  sudo apt install nmap
  nmap -v
  ```

- **apt remove: Removing Packages (Leaving Configuration Files)**

  The apt remove package_name command removes a package from your system, but it leaves the configuration files associated with the package intact. This is useful if you want to remove the software but keep its settings for future use.

  ```
  sudo apt remove wireshark
  ```

- **apt purge: Erasing All Traces**

The apt purge package_name command removes a package and its configuration files. This is a more thorough removal process that ensures that all traces of the software are removed from your system.

```
sudo apt purge wireshark
```

Practical Example:

1. Run sudo apt install wireshark.
2. Run sudo apt purge wireshark.
3. Verify that Wireshark has been removed and that its configuration files have been deleted.

```
sudo apt install wireshark
sudo apt purge wireshark
```

- **apt search: Finding the Right Tool**

The apt search package_name command searches for packages that match a specific keyword or name. This is useful if you're not sure of the exact name of the package you want to install.

```
apt search network-scanner
```

This command searches for packages related to network scanning.

Practical Example:

1. Run apt search password manager.
2. Observe the output, which shows a list of packages related to password management.

```
apt search password manager
```

- **apt show: Getting the Details**

The apt show package_name command displays detailed information about a specific package, including its name, version, description, dependencies, and other metadata.

```
apt show nmap
```

This command shows information about the Nmap network scanner.

Practical Example:

1. Run apt show nmap.
2. Observe the output, which shows detailed information about the Nmap package.

```
apt show nmap
```

[Insight: I always use apt show before installing a new package to get a better understanding of what it does and what dependencies it requires.]

Practical Scenario: Setting Up a Penetration Testing Lab

Let's say you're setting up a penetration testing lab and you need to install several common tools:

1. Update the package lists:

```
sudo apt update
```

2. Install Nmap, Metasploit Framework, and Wireshark:

```
sudo apt install nmap metasploit-framework wireshark
```

3. Verify that the tools have been installed correctly by running them:

```
nmap -v
msfconsole
wireshark
```

Keeping Your System Secure: A Continuous Process

Package management is not a one-time task. It's an ongoing process that you should perform regularly to keep your system secure and up-to-date. I suggest running apt update and apt upgrade at least once a week, or even more frequently if you're working on a security-sensitive system.

Troubleshooting: When Things Go Wrong

Sometimes, package management can run into problems. Here are some common issues and how to resolve them:

- **Broken Dependencies:** This occurs when a package requires another package that is not available or is incompatible. Try running sudo apt --fix-broken install to resolve the dependencies.
- **Package Conflicts:** This occurs when two packages conflict with each other. Try removing one of the conflicting packages or using a different package management tool.
- **Repository Errors:** This occurs when there is a problem with the software repositories. Check your internet connection and verify that the repository addresses are correct.

[Insight I've spent countless hours troubleshooting package management issues. The key is to stay calm, read the error messages carefully, and search online for solutions. The Linux community is incredibly helpful, and you're likely to find someone who has experienced the same problem and can offer advice.]

Chapter 3: Networking Essentials: Connecting the Dots in the Digital World

Welcome to the world of networking! This chapter is all about building a solid understanding of the fundamental concepts that underpin how computers communicate with each other. Think of it like learning the rules of the road before you start driving. Without this foundational knowledge, it will be hard to use advanced tools or even exploit vulnerabilities. We'll be covering IP addresses, subnetting, DNS, essential protocols like TCP/IP, HTTP, and SSH, how to configure network interfaces, how to use basic tools like ping and traceroute, and understanding how network services operate.

3.1 Networking Fundamentals: IP Addresses, Subnets, DNS: Laying the Foundation for Network Mastery

Before we can even *think* about exploiting vulnerabilities or analyzing network traffic, we need to grasp the fundamental concepts that make it all possible. Think of IP addresses, subnets, and DNS as the foundation upon which the entire internet (and many private networks) are built. Without a solid understanding of these concepts, you'll be lost in the weeds.

IP Addresses: Giving Each Device a Unique Identity

Imagine trying to deliver mail without addresses. Chaos, right? IP addresses serve the same purpose on a network: they provide a unique identifier for each device, allowing other devices to find and communicate with it.

There are two main versions of IP addresses in use today: IPv4 and IPv6.

- **IPv4: The Veteran**

  IPv4 (Internet Protocol version 4) is the older of the two. It uses a 32-bit address, typically represented in dotted decimal notation. For example: 192.168.1.100.

  Each of the four numbers can range from 0 to 255. This gives IPv4 a theoretical maximum of around 4.3 billion unique addresses. While that seemed like a lot back in the day, it's nowhere near enough to accommodate the billions of devices connected to the internet today.

  That's why IPv6 was created.

- **IPv6: The New Kid on the Block**

  IPv6 (Internet Protocol version 6) uses a 128-bit address, represented in hexadecimal notation. For example: 2001:0db8:85a3:0000:0000:8a2e:0370:7334.

  This vastly increases the number of available addresses to a staggering 3.4 x 10^38, which should be enough to last us for a very, very long time.

  IPv6 also includes several other improvements over IPv4, such as improved security and simplified address configuration.

[Personal Insight Placeholder 1: When I first started learning about networking, I found IPv6 addresses incredibly intimidating. All those colons and hexadecimal numbers! But once you understand the structure, it becomes much easier to work with.]

Practical Exercises: Finding Your IP Address

Let's see how to find your IP address on Kali Linux:

1. **Using ip addr show:**

   This command is the modern way to display network interface information.

   ```
   ip addr show
   ```

   Look for your network interface (e.g., eth0, wlan0) and the inet entry, which shows your IPv4 address. The inet6 shows the IPv6 address if the interface is configured for IPv6.
   The device may have multiple IP addresses.

2. **Using ifconfig:**

   This command is an older, but still common, way to display network interface information.

   ```
   ifconfig
   ```

   Look for your network interface and the inet addr entry, which shows your IPv4 address. Again, this might not be installed and will require addition via APT.

   Interpreting the Output:

   The output of these commands will show you a lot of information about your network interfaces, including:

   - **Interface name:** (e.g., eth0, wlan0, lo)
   - **IP address:** (e.g., 192.168.1.100, 2001:db8::1)
   - **Netmask:** (e.g., 255.255.255.0, /64)
   - **Broadcast address:** (e.g., 192.168.1.255)

- **MAC address:** (e.g., 00:11:22:33:44:55)

Public vs. Private IP Addresses: Staying Secure

Not all IP addresses are created equal. There are public IP addresses and private IP addresses.

- **Public IP Addresses: Facing the World**

  Public IP addresses are used for communication on the public internet. They are unique across the entire internet. Your internet service provider (ISP) assigns these, and you can learn it using tools like whatismyip.com.

- **Private IP Addresses: Staying Inside the Network**

  Private IP addresses are used for communication within a private network, such as your home or office network. They are *not* unique across the entire internet.

  Private IP addresses are defined in the following ranges:

  - 10.0.0.0 - 10.255.255.255
  - 172.16.0.0 - 172.31.255.255
  - 192.168.0.0 - 192.168.255.255

  Devices on your private network use these addresses to communicate with each other. When they need to communicate with the outside world, they use a technique called Network Address Translation (NAT) to translate their private IP address to your public IP address. NAT creates a secure barrier.

- **The Loopback IP Address**

A special IP address also exists which allows a machine to communicate with itself. This IP is commonly referred to as "localhost" and is 127.0.0.1.

Subnets: Dividing and Conquering Networks

Subnets allow you to divide a large network into smaller, more manageable segments. This improves network performance and security.

Imagine you have a large office building with hundreds of employees. It would be difficult to manage everyone if they were all on the same network. Subnets allow you to divide the office into departments, with each department having its own network segment.

- **Subnet Masks: Defining the Boundaries**

  A subnet mask is used to identify the network portion and the host portion of an IP address. It's a 32-bit number that is typically represented in dotted decimal notation. For example: 255.255.255.0.

  The 1 bits in the subnet mask represent the network portion of the IP address, and the 0 bits represent the host portion.

  For example, if you have an IP address of 192.168.1.100 and a subnet mask of 255.255.255.0, the network portion of the IP address is 192.168.1.0, and the host portion is 100.

- **CIDR Notation: A Shorter Way to Write It**

  CIDR (Classless Inter-Domain Routing) notation is a more compact way to represent subnet masks. It specifies the number of bits in the network portion of the IP address.

  For example, 192.168.1.100/24 is equivalent to 192.168.1.100 with a subnet mask of 255.255.255.0. The /24 indicates that the first 24 bits of the IP address are the network portion.

  CIDR notation makes it easier to reason about subnets and network sizes.

  To understand this:

  - A /32 network has 2^0 = 1 address (host only)
  - A /31 network has 2^1 = 2 addresses
  - A /30 network has 2^2 = 4 addresses (two usable). Usable addresses are network address + 1 and broadcast address -1.

  What is a network and broadcast address? The range starts with the network address (the first IP in the range) and ends with the broadcast address (the last IP in the range). For example, with a 192.168.1.0/24 network:

  - 192.168.1.0 is the network address
  - 192.168.1.255 is the broadcast address

- 192.168.1.1 - 192.168.1.254 are the "usable" addresses for machines to communicate.

A /24 gives 2^8 addresses = 256 addresses.

DNS: Translating Names to Numbers

Humans prefer to use names (like google.com), but computers communicate using numbers (IP addresses). DNS (Domain Name System) bridges this gap by translating domain names into IP addresses. Think of it as the internet's phone book.

When you type google.com into your web browser, your computer sends a DNS query to a DNS server. The DNS server then looks up the corresponding IP address (e.g., 142.250.184.78) and returns it to your computer. Your computer then uses the IP address to connect to the web server.

- **DNS Hierarchy: A Global Network**

  DNS is organized in a hierarchical structure:

  - **Root Servers:** The top-level servers in the DNS hierarchy. They know where to find the TLD servers.
  - **Top-Level Domain (TLD) Servers:** Manage the top-level domains, such as .com, .org, and .net. They know where to find the authoritative name servers for specific domains.
  - **Authoritative Name Servers:** Hold the actual DNS records for specific domains.
  - **Recursive DNS Servers (Resolvers):** Handle DNS queries from clients, caching responses to speed up future lookups. These are typically provided by your ISP or a public DNS service like Google DNS (8.8.8.8) or Cloudflare DNS (1.1.1.1).
- **DNS Records: The Key Information**

  DNS records contain information about a domain, such as its IP address, mail servers, and other settings.

  Some common DNS record types include:

  - **A Record:** Maps a domain name to an IPv4 address.
  - **AAAA Record:** Maps a domain name to an IPv6 address.
  - **MX Record:** Specifies the mail servers for a domain.
  - **CNAME Record:** Creates an alias for a domain name.

- **NS Record:** Specifies the name servers for a domain.

Practical Exercise: Querying DNS Servers

Let's use the nslookup command to query DNS servers and find the IP address associated with a domain name:

1. **Open a terminal.**
2. **Run nslookup google.com:**

```
nslookup google.com
```

The output will show you the IP address(es) associated with google.com, as well as the DNS server that was used to perform the lookup.

3. **Run dig google.com:**

```
dig google.com
```

The output will show more information, including the IP address(es) associated with google.com, the DNS server that was used to perform the lookup, and more.

If you do not have either of these commands installed, you may need to do so via APT.

[Personal Insight Placeholder 2: I often use DNS lookups to verify that my DNS settings are configured correctly. It's a quick way to troubleshoot DNS-related issues.]

In summary:

IP addresses, subnets, and DNS are fundamental concepts that underpin all network communication. Without a solid understanding of these concepts, you'll be lost. With this knowledge, you are well-equipped to troubleshoot network issues, configure network interfaces, and explore more advanced networking topics.

3.2 Network Protocols: TCP/IP, HTTP, SSH: Understanding the Conversation

We've covered the basics of addressing, but how do computers actually *talk* to each other? That's where network protocols come in. Think of these as the languages that computers use to communicate. Without understanding these protocols, you are just listening to noise. In this section, we will dissect three key protocols: TCP/IP, HTTP, and SSH.

TCP/IP: The Foundation of Internet Communication

TCP/IP (Transmission Control Protocol/Internet Protocol) isn't just one protocol; it's a suite of protocols that forms the foundation of the internet. It defines how data is broken down into packets, transmitted across networks, and reassembled at the destination. TCP/IP is the backbone of how data moves.

Imagine sending a letter across the country. You wouldn't just write the letter and throw it out the window, right? You'd put it in an envelope, address it correctly, and send it through the postal system. TCP/IP does something similar for data on the internet.

- **The Layered Model: A Hierarchical Approach**

  TCP/IP is based on a layered model, with each layer responsible for a specific function:

  1. **Application Layer:** This is the layer closest to the user. It provides network services to applications, such as web browsers, email clients, and file transfer programs. Protocols like HTTP, SSH, FTP, and SMTP reside in this layer.
  2. **Transport Layer:** This layer provides reliable and unreliable data transfer between applications. The two main protocols in this layer are TCP and UDP.
     - **TCP (Transmission Control Protocol):** Provides reliable, connection-oriented communication. It ensures that data is delivered in the correct order and without errors. TCP is used for applications that require reliable data transfer, such as web browsing, email, and file transfer.
     - **UDP (User Datagram Protocol):** Provides unreliable, connectionless communication. It does not guarantee that data will be delivered in the correct order or without errors. UDP

is used for applications that require speed and low latency, such as streaming video, online gaming, and DNS.

3. **Internet Layer:** This layer handles addressing and routing of packets between networks. The main protocol in this layer is IP (Internet Protocol). IP is responsible for assigning IP addresses to devices and routing packets to their destination.
4. **Link Layer:** This layer handles the physical transmission of data over the network. It includes protocols such as Ethernet, Wi-Fi, and PPP. The data is translated to electrical pulses for transmission.

This layered approach allows each layer to focus on its specific function without worrying about the details of the other layers. It's like having different departments in a company, each responsible for a specific task.

[Personal Insight Placeholder 1: Understanding the TCP/IP layered model is essential for troubleshooting network issues. By identifying which layer is causing the problem, you can quickly narrow down the possible causes.]

Practical Implementation:

While you don't directly "use" TCP/IP in the command line, you can observe its behavior using tools like Wireshark. Wireshark will show you the different layers of the TCP/IP model and how data is encapsulated as it travels across the network. The headers can be easily read.

1. Install Wireshark

```
sudo apt install wireshark
```

2. Run Wireshark and capture traffic by specifying which interface you want to listen to

HTTP: The Voice of the Web

HTTP (Hypertext Transfer Protocol) is the protocol used for transferring data over the web. It defines how web browsers and web servers communicate with each other.

When you type a URL into your web browser, your browser sends an HTTP request to the web server. The web server then responds with an HTTP response, which contains the requested web page or resource (HTML, images, CSS, etc.).

- **Key Concepts: Requests and Responses**

  HTTP communication is based on a request-response model:

  - **HTTP Request:** A message sent from a client (e.g., web browser) to a server, requesting a specific resource or action.
  - **HTTP Response:** A message sent from a server to a client in response to an HTTP request. It contains the requested resource (or an error message).
- **HTTP Methods: Different Ways to Interact**

  HTTP defines several methods (also known as verbs) for performing different actions on a web server:

  - **GET:** Retrieves a resource from the server. This is the most common method.
  - **POST:** Sends data to the server to create or update a resource. Used for submitting forms or uploading files.
  - **PUT:** Replaces an existing resource with new data.
  - **DELETE:** Deletes a resource.
  - **PATCH:** Partially modifies a resource.
  - **HEAD:** Retrieves the headers of a resource without retrieving the body.
  - **OPTIONS:** Describes the communication options for the target resource.
- **HTTP Status Codes: Understanding the Outcome**

  HTTP status codes are three-digit numbers that indicate the outcome of an HTTP request. They provide valuable information about whether the request was successful, encountered an error, or requires further action.

  - **200 OK:** The request was successful. The server returned the requested resource.
  - **301 Moved Permanently:** The requested resource has been permanently moved to a new location.
  - **400 Bad Request:** The server cannot understand the request due to malformed syntax.
  - **401 Unauthorized:** The request requires authentication.
  - **403 Forbidden:** The server refuses to fulfill the request, even if the client is authenticated.
  - **404 Not Found:** The requested resource could not be found on the server.

- **500 Internal Server Error:** The server encountered an unexpected error.

- **HTTPS: Securing the Web**

  HTTPS (HTTP Secure) is a secure version of HTTP that uses encryption to protect data transmitted between the web browser and the web server. HTTPS uses TLS (Transport Layer Security) or SSL (Secure Sockets Layer) to encrypt the communication, preventing eavesdropping and tampering.

  You can tell if a website is using HTTPS by looking for the padlock icon in the address bar of your web browser. The web address also begins with https:// instead of http://.

Practical Implementation:

You can interact with HTTP servers from the command line using tools like curl and wget. This allows you to send HTTP requests and examine the responses.

1. **Using curl to retrieve a web page:**

   ```
   curl https://www.example.com
   ```

   This command will retrieve the HTML source code of the www.example.com web page and display it in your terminal. You can also add the -I to only return the header and not the contents of the page.

2. **Using curl to view the HTTP headers:**

   ```
   curl -I https://www.example.com
   ```

   This command will retrieve the HTTP headers from www.example.com and display them in your terminal. The headers provide valuable information about the server, the content type, and other settings.

3. **Using wget to download a file:**

   ```
   wget https://www.example.com/image.jpg
   ```

   This command will download the file image.jpg from www.example.com and save it to your current directory.

You can also easily create your own tools to query the web.

SSH: Your Secure Remote Control

SSH (Secure Shell) is a cryptographic network protocol for securely accessing a remote computer. It provides a secure channel over an unsecured network.

Imagine you want to access your server from a remote location. You wouldn't want to send your username and password in plain text over the internet, right? SSH encrypts all data transmitted between the client and the server, protecting your credentials and sensitive information.

- **Key Features:**
  - **Encryption:** SSH uses strong encryption algorithms to protect data from eavesdropping.
  - **Authentication:** SSH supports multiple authentication methods, including passwords, public keys, and Kerberos.
  - **Port Forwarding:** SSH allows you to forward ports between your local machine and the remote server, creating secure tunnels for other applications.
  - **Secure File Transfer:** SSH can be used to securely transfer files between your local machine and the remote server using the scp command.
- **Common Uses:**

  SSH is commonly used for:

  - Remote command-line access
  - Secure file transfer
  - Port forwarding
  - Managing remote servers

Practical Implementation:

1. **Connecting to a remote server using SSH:**

   ```
   ssh username@remote_server
   ```

   Replace username with your username on the remote server and remote_server with the IP address or hostname of the remote server.

2. **Securely copying files to a remote server using scp:**

   ```
   scp myfile.txt username@remote_server:/path/to/destination
   ```

   This command copies myfile.txt to the /path/to/destination directory on the remote server.

3. **Using SSH port forwarding to access a local service on a remote server:**

   ```
   ssh -L 8080:localhost:80 username@remote_server
   ```

   This command forwards port 8080 on your local machine to port 80 on the remote server. You can then access the web server running on the remote server by browsing to http://localhost:8080 in your web browser.

Documentation Style:

- **Comments:** Add comments to your code to explain what it does and why.
- **Variable Names:** Use meaningful variable names to improve readability.
- **Indentation:** Use consistent indentation to make your code easier to follow.

You should now be able to differentiate the protocols, explain the layers, and start interacting using tools from the command line. We can dig deeper into specific aspects, or perhaps move on?

3.3 Network Configuration: ifconfig / ip, Configuration Files: Making the Connection

In the previous section, we discussed protocols. However, before any data can be transmitted or received, your network interface needs to be properly configured. This involves assigning an IP address, subnet mask, and gateway address to your network interface. Think of it as setting up your postal address before you can receive mail. This section will cover how to do this using both the legacy ifconfig tool and the modern ip command.

Choosing Your Tool: ifconfig vs. ip

Historically, ifconfig (interface configuration) was the standard tool for configuring network interfaces on Linux systems. However, it has been largely superseded by the ip (IP Route2) command on most modern distributions.

While ifconfig is still available on many systems, it is considered deprecated and may not be supported in the future. The ip command offers more features and flexibility, and it is the preferred tool for network configuration on modern Linux distributions.

For the sake of completeness, we will cover both ifconfig and ip in this section. However, we recommend that you focus on learning the ip command, as it is the more modern and widely used tool.

Inspecting Your Interfaces: Discovering What's Out There

Before we can configure anything, we need to know what network interfaces are available on your system. You can use either ifconfig or ip to display information about your network interfaces.

- **Using ifconfig:**

  ```
  ifconfig
  ```

  This command will display information about all active network interfaces.

  The output will show you a lot of information, including:

  - Interface name (e.g., eth0, wlan0, lo)
  - IP address (inet addr)
  - Subnet mask (Mask)
  - MAC address (HWaddr)

  The lo interface is the loopback interface, which is used for communication within your local system. It always has the IP address 127.0.0.1.

  [Personal Insight Placeholder 1: I used to rely heavily on ifconfig, but I've since switched to ip. It's just more powerful and flexible, and it provides a lot more information.]

- **Using ip:**

```
ip addr show
```

This command displays information about all network interfaces, including both active and inactive interfaces.

The output will show you a lot of information, including:

- Interface name
- IP address (inet)
- Subnet mask (cidr notation after the IP address)
- MAC address (link/ether)

Configuring an Interface: Assigning Addresses and More

Now that we know how to inspect our interfaces, let's learn how to configure them. This involves assigning an IP address, subnet mask, and gateway address to your network interface.

- **Using ifconfig (Temporary Configuration):**

  The ifconfig command can be used to temporarily configure a network interface. These changes will be lost when you reboot your system. This is useful for testing or for situations where you need to change your network configuration temporarily.

  To assign an IP address and subnet mask to an interface:

  ```
  sudo ifconfig eth0 192.168.1.100 netmask 255.255.255.0
  ```

  Replace eth0 with the name of your network interface and 192.168.1.100 and 255.255.255.0 with the desired IP address and subnet mask.

  To bring the interface up (enable it):

  ```
  sudo ifconfig eth0 up
  ```

  To bring the interface down (disable it):

  ```
  sudo ifconfig eth0 down
  ```

- **Using ip (Temporary Configuration):**

  The ip command can also be used to temporarily configure a network interface. These changes will also be lost when you reboot your system.

  To assign an IP address and subnet mask to an interface:

```
sudo ip addr add 192.168.1.100/24 dev eth0
```

  Replace eth0 with the name of your network interface and 192.168.1.100/24 with the desired IP address and subnet mask in CIDR notation.

  To bring the interface up (enable it):

```
sudo ip link set dev eth0 up
```

  To bring the interface down (disable it):

```
sudo ip link set dev eth0 down
```

  To remove an IP address from an interface:

```
sudo ip addr del 192.168.1.100/24 dev eth0
```

Persisting Your Changes: Editing Configuration Files

The changes we've made so far are temporary. To make them permanent, we need to edit the network configuration files. The location and format of these files vary depending on your Linux distribution.

On Debian-based systems (like Kali Linux), the network configuration files are typically located in the /etc/network/interfaces directory.

Editing /etc/network/interfaces (Debian-based Systems):

1. Open the /etc/network/interfaces file in a text editor with root privileges:

```
sudo nano /etc/network/interfaces
```

This opens the file using the nano text editor, with administrative privileges.

2. Add or modify the configuration for your network interface.

   Here are some common configurations:

   - **DHCP (Dynamic Host Configuration Protocol):**

     DHCP is a protocol that automatically assigns IP addresses and other network settings to devices on a network. This is the most common configuration for home networks.

     To configure an interface to use DHCP, add the following lines to the /etc/network/interfaces file:

```
auto eth0
iface eth0 inet dhcp
```

   - **Static IP Address:**

     A static IP address is a fixed IP address that is manually assigned to a device. This is useful for servers or other devices that need to have a consistent IP address.

     To configure an interface to use a static IP address, add the following lines to the /etc/network/interfaces file:

```
   auto eth0
iface eth0 inet static
    address 192.168.1.100
    netmask 255.255.255.0
    gateway 192.168.1.1
    dns-nameservers 8.8.8.8 8.8.4.4
```

     Replace 192.168.1.100 with the desired IP address, 255.255.255.0 with the subnet mask, 192.168.1.1 with the gateway address, and 8.8.8.8 and 8.8.4.4 with the DNS server addresses.

3. Save the file and exit the text editor.

   In nano, press Ctrl+X, then Y, then Enter to save and exit.

4. Restart the networking service for the changes to take effect:

```
sudo systemctl restart networking
```

This will restart the networking service, and your new network configuration should be applied.

Important Notes:

- Always make a backup of your network configuration files before making any changes.
- Be careful when editing the network configuration files, as incorrect settings can prevent your system from connecting to the network.
- If you are using a graphical network manager, such as NetworkManager, you may need to disable it before editing the network configuration files.

Documenting the Commands:

```
# Display network interface information using ip
ip addr show
# Set the IP address of eth0 to 192.168.0.5 and netmask to
255.255.255.0
sudo ip addr add 192.168.0.5/24 dev eth0
# Bring the eth0 up
sudo ip link set dev eth0 up
# Set the default gateway
sudo ip route add default via 192.168.0.1
# View the routing table
ip route show
# Add the Google DNS servers to resolv.conf
echo "nameserver 8.8.8.8" | sudo tee /etc/resolv.conf
echo "nameserver 8.8.4.4" | sudo tee -a /etc/resolv.conf
```

Caveats:

- When troubleshooting, always double check physical connections
- Make sure your networking configuration changes persist through reboots

What do you think? Are you ready to connect or do you want to work on this some more?

3.4 Common Network Tools: ping, traceroute, netstat / ss: Become a Network Detective

You now know how to configure your network interface. But what happens when things go wrong? How do you diagnose network issues and figure out what's preventing you from connecting to a remote host? This section introduces you to essential network tools: ping, traceroute, netstat, and ss. Think of these as your detective kit for solving network mysteries.

ping: The Basic Connectivity Check

The ping command is your first line of defense when troubleshooting network connectivity. It sends ICMP (Internet Control Message Protocol) echo requests to a remote host and waits for a response. This tells you whether the host is reachable and how long it takes for a packet to travel to the host and back.

```
ping google.com
```

This command sends ICMP echo requests to google.com.

- **Interpreting the Output:**

  The output of the ping command will show you the following information:

  - **Round-trip time (RTT):** The time it takes for a packet to travel to the host and back, in milliseconds. Lower RTT values indicate better connectivity.
  - **Packet loss:** The percentage of packets that were lost during the ping test. Higher packet loss values indicate poor connectivity or network congestion.
  - **Sequence number (icmp_seq):** The number of the ICMP echo request packet being sent. This increments with each successive ping.
- **Common Options:**
  - -c count: Specifies the number of ping packets to send.

    ```
    ping -c 4 google.com
    ```

  - -i interval: Specifies the interval between ping packets, in seconds.

    ```
    ping -i 2 google.com
    ```

- **Practical Scenarios:**
    1. **Check basic connectivity to the internet:**

       ```
       ping 8.8.8.8  # Google's public DNS server
       ```

       If you can ping 8.8.8.8, it means your system has basic connectivity to the internet.

    2. **Check connectivity to a local device:**

       ```
       ping 192.168.1.100  # Replace with the IP address of your local device
       ```

       If you can ping the local device, it means your system can communicate with the device on your local network.

    3. **Troubleshoot DNS resolution:**

       ```
       ping google.com
       ```

       If you can ping 8.8.8.8 but cannot ping google.com, it may indicate a problem with DNS resolution. This means you need to address DNS configuration.

- *:use ping all the time to quickly check if a server is online. It's a simple but effective way to diagnose connectivity issues.]*

traceroute: Mapping the Network Path

The traceroute command traces the route that packets take to reach a remote host. It shows the IP addresses of each router along the path. This can be useful for identifying network bottlenecks or connectivity issues.

```
traceroute google.com
```

This command traces the route to google.com.

- **Interpreting the Output:**

  The output of the traceroute command will show you the following information:

  - **Hop number:** The number of each hop along the path.
  - **Hostname or IP address:** The hostname or IP address of the router at each hop.
  - **Round-trip time (RTT):** The time it takes for a packet to travel to each hop and back, in milliseconds.
- **Practical Scenarios:**
  1. **Identify network bottlenecks:**

     If you notice high RTT values at a particular hop, it may indicate a network bottleneck at that location.

  2. **Identify routing loops:**

     If the traceroute output shows the same IP address appearing multiple times, it may indicate a routing loop.

  3. **Verify the path that packets are taking:**

     Traceroute can be used to verify that packets are taking the expected path to reach a remote host.

     ```
     traceroute example.com
     ```
-

netstat / ss: Examining Network Connections and Listening Ports

The netstat (network statistics) command displays information about network connections, routing tables, and interface statistics. However, netstat is being phased out in favor of the ss (socket statistics) command on many modern Linux distributions.

Both commands provide similar functionality, but ss is generally faster and more efficient.

- **netstat (Legacy Tool):**

```
netstat -an  # Display all active network connections and
listening ports
netstat -rn  # Display the routing table
netstat -i   # Display interface statistics
```

- **ss (Modern Tool):**

```
      ss -an   # Display all active network connections and
listening ports
ss -rn   # Display the routing table
ss -i    # Display interface statistics
```

- **Key Information:**

  The output of these commands will show you a lot of information, including:

  - **Local Address:** The IP address and port number of your system.
  - **Foreign Address:** The IP address and port number of the remote host.
  - **State:** The state of the connection (e.g., ESTABLISHED, LISTEN, TIME_WAIT).
  - **PID/Program name:** The process ID and name of the program associated with the connection.
- **Practical Scenarios:**
  1. **Identify listening ports:**

     You can use netstat -an or ss -an to see which ports are listening for incoming connections on your system. This is useful for identifying services that are running on your system.

     If your system is running a web server, it will typically be listening on port 80 (HTTP) or port 443 (HTTPS).

  2. **Identify established connections:**

     You can use netstat -an or ss -an to see which connections are currently established on your system. This can be useful for identifying malicious connections or for troubleshooting network performance issues.

  3. **View the routing table:**

You can use netstat -rn or ss -rn to view the routing table, which shows how packets are routed to different destinations. This is useful for troubleshooting routing problems.

4. List ports in listening state.

```
sudo ss -ltnp

*   -l, --listening: Display only listening sockets.
*   -t, --tcp: Display only TCP sockets.
*   -n, --numeric: Show numeric port numbers.
*   -p, --processes: Show the PID and name of the
process to which each socket belongs.
```

```
*[Personal Insight Placeholder 2: I use `netstat` and `ss` all the
time to investigate network connections and identify potential
security threats. It's essential to understand what services are
running on your system and how they are communicating with the
outside world.]*
```

A Practical Scenario: Troubleshooting a Web Server Connection

Let's say you're trying to access a web server on a remote host, but you're getting a "Connection timed out" error. Here's how you could use these tools to diagnose the problem:

1. **Ping the remote host:**

   ```
   ping remote_host
   ```

   If you can't ping the remote host, it means there's a basic connectivity problem. Check your network connection, your DNS settings, and the firewall settings on both your system and the remote host.

2. **Traceroute to the remote host:**

   ```
   traceroute remote_host
   ```

   If you can ping the remote host but you're still getting a "Connection timed out" error, use traceroute to identify any network bottlenecks or routing loops along the path.

3. **Check for listening ports on the remote host:**

   If you can ping the remote host and traceroute doesn't show any obvious problems, use netstat or ss to check if the web server is listening on the expected port (80 for HTTP, 443 for HTTPS). You'll need to run these commands on the remote host.
   In order to test a remote host, you will need to connect to that host using ssh.

Documentation Style:

- **Comments:** Add comments to your code to explain what it does and why.
- **Variable Names:** Use meaningful variable names to improve readability.
- **Indentation:** Use consistent indentation to make your code easier to follow.

You are now at a point where you can test connectivity, examine the network path, and view the programs that are connected. This is a good start in network analysis. Ready to move on?

3.5 Understanding Network Services & Ports: The Keys to the Kingdom

You've learned how to check connectivity and diagnose network issues. Now, let's delve into the heart of network communication: understanding network services and the ports they use. Think of network services as the applications running on a server, and ports as the virtual doorways through which those applications communicate. Knowing which services run on which ports is crucial for both attacking and defending systems.

Network Services: What's Running in the Background?

Network services are applications that provide specific functionality over a network. They are the workhorses of the internet, providing everything from web pages and email to file sharing and remote access.

Some common network services include:

- **Web servers (HTTP/HTTPS):** Serve web pages and other content to web browsers.
- **Email servers (SMTP/IMAP/POP3):** Send and receive email messages.
- **File servers (FTP/SFTP/NFS/SMB):** Allow users to share files over the network.

- **DNS servers (DNS):** Translate domain names into IP addresses.
- **Database servers (MySQL/PostgreSQL):** Store and manage data.
- **SSH servers (SSH):** Provide secure remote access to the system.

These services often run in the background. You are using them without even knowing!

Ports: The Virtual Doorways

Ports are numerical identifiers that allow different applications on the same device to communicate with each other. Think of them as apartment numbers in a building. Each apartment number represents a different application, and the street address represents the IP address of the building.

Ports are 16-bit numbers, ranging from 0 to 65535.

- **Well-Known Ports (0-1023): The Standard Entryways**

  These ports are reserved for well-known services and are typically used by system-level processes. They are assigned and managed by the Internet Assigned Numbers Authority (IANA).

  Some common well-known ports include:

  - **20/21: FTP (File Transfer Protocol):** Used for transferring files between computers.
  - **22: SSH (Secure Shell):** Used for secure remote access to the system.
  - **23: Telnet:** Used for unencrypted remote access to the system (less secure than SSH).
  - **25: SMTP (Simple Mail Transfer Protocol):** Used for sending email messages.
  - **53: DNS (Domain Name System):** Used for translating domain names into IP addresses.
  - **80: HTTP (Hypertext Transfer Protocol):** Used for transferring web pages and other content over the internet.
  - **110: POP3 (Post Office Protocol version 3):** Used for retrieving email messages from a server.
  - **143: IMAP (Internet Message Access Protocol):** Used for retrieving and managing email messages on a server.
  - **443: HTTPS (HTTP Secure):** The secured version of HTTP.

You can find a comprehensive list of well-known ports in the /etc/services file on your Linux system. This file maps port numbers to service names. This file contains a mapping between port numbers and the services that typically use them. While not always definitive, it provides a useful reference.

```
less /etc/services
```

- **Registered Ports (1024-49151): The Application Zone**

  These ports are registered with IANA and can be used by applications to provide specific services. However, they are not as tightly controlled as well-known ports, and some applications may use them without registering.

  - 3306 MySQL database system
  - 5432 PostgreSQL database system
  - 8080 often used as an alternate web port
- **Dynamic/Private Ports (49152-65535): The Ephemeral Ports**

  These ports are not assigned to any specific service and are typically used for temporary connections. They are often used by client applications when communicating with servers.

  [Personal Insight Placeholder 1: Knowing the common port numbers for different services is essential for penetration testing. It allows you to quickly identify potential targets and focus your efforts on the most likely attack vectors.]

Listing Listening Ports: What's Open for Business?

A listening port is a port on which a service is waiting for incoming connections. You can use the netstat or ss command to see which services are listening on which ports.

- **Using netstat (Legacy):**

```
sudo netstat -tulnp
```

- **Using ss (Modern):**

```
sudo ss -tulnp
```

The output of these commands will show you the following information:

- **Proto:** The protocol used by the service (TCP or UDP).
- **Local Address:** The IP address and port number on which the service is listening.
- **Foreign Address:** The IP address and port number of the remote host (if the connection is established).
- **State:** The state of the connection (e.g., LISTEN, ESTABLISHED).
- **PID/Program name:** The process ID and name of the program associated with the service.

Let's break down what each option means:

```
sudo ss -tulnp
```

Here is breakdown of this command:

- sudo: This means you are running the command with superuser privileges. This is necessary because viewing detailed information about network sockets often requires elevated permissions.
- ss: This is the command itself, which stands for "socket statistics". It is used to display network socket-related information.
- -t: This option is used to filter and display only TCP sockets (Transmission Control Protocol). TCP is a connection-oriented protocol that provides reliable, ordered, and error-checked delivery of a stream of data.
- -u: This option is used to filter and display only UDP sockets (User Datagram Protocol). UDP is a connectionless protocol that provides a faster but less reliable method of transmitting data, often used for streaming or DNS queries.
- -l: This option is used to list only listening sockets. A listening socket is one that is actively waiting for incoming connections.
- -n: This option is used to display port numbers numerically rather than attempting to resolve them to service names.
- -p: This option is used to show the process ID (PID) and name of the program to which each socket belongs. This can help you identify which application is using a particular socket.

Firewalls: Protecting Your Ports

Firewalls are essential security tools that control network traffic, allowing only authorized connections and blocking everything else. They act as a gatekeeper, protecting your system from unauthorized access.

Firewalls work by examining network traffic and comparing it to a set of rules. If the traffic matches a rule, the firewall will take the appropriate action, such as allowing or blocking the connection.

Some popular Linux firewalls include:

- iptables: A powerful but complex firewall that is built into the Linux kernel.
- ufw: A user-friendly front-end for iptables that simplifies the process of configuring the firewall.

Practical Scenario: Identifying Open Ports and Services

Let's say you want to identify the open ports and services running on a remote server. You can use Nmap. This is a security tool and will be explored later.

1. **Scan the remote host using Nmap:**

   ```
   nmap -sV -p 1-100 remote_host
   ```

   Replace remote_host with the IP address or hostname of the remote server.

   The -sV option tells Nmap to perform version detection, which attempts to identify the software version of each service running on the open ports. The -p 1-100 options tell Nmap to scan ports 1-100.

2. Open the report and examine the open ports and services. Nmap can also be configured to scan all ports, but that will take much longer.

- To review the syntax of other ports, use this command:

  ```
  nmap -h
  ```

Practical Scenario: Securing a Web Server

Suppose you are securing a web server and want to ensure that only HTTP (port 80) and HTTPS (port 443) traffic are allowed. You can use ufw to configure the firewall:

1. **Enable ufw:**

```
sudo ufw enable
```

2. **Allow HTTP and HTTPS traffic:**

```
sudo ufw allow 80
sudo ufw allow 443
```

3. **Deny all other incoming traffic:**

```
sudo ufw default deny incoming
```

4. **Check the firewall status:**

```
sudo ufw status
```

This will display the current firewall rules.

[Personal Insight Placeholder 2: I've seen countless systems compromised because of misconfigured firewalls or unnecessary services running on open ports. It's essential to minimize the attack surface by disabling unnecessary services and carefully configuring your firewall rules.]

What to Do Next:

Chapter 4: Network Scanning & Reconnaissance: Gathering Intelligence Like a Pro

Now that you understand the fundamentals of networking, it's time to learn how to gather information about networks and systems. Think of this chapter as learning how to scout ahead before launching an attack (or a defense!). This process, known as reconnaissance, involves gathering information about the target network, including identifying active hosts, open ports, running services, and operating systems. This chapter covers tools to do this such as Nmap, Wireshark, and tcpdump, and also how to use passive reconnaissance to gather information.

4.1 Introduction to Network Scanning: Mapping Out the Territory

Before you can even think about exploiting vulnerabilities or testing security measures, you need to understand the terrain. In the world of cybersecurity, that terrain is the network. Network scanning is the process of discovering the devices (hosts), services, and operating systems present on a network. It's like reconnaissance for a penetration tester, ethical hacker, or even a sysadmin trying to secure their environment.

Why Scan? Unveiling the Network's Secrets

Think of a network as a city. To understand its strengths and weaknesses, you need to explore it, identify its key infrastructure, and understand how everything is connected. Network scanning provides that level of understanding.

Here's why network scanning is crucial:

- **Identifying Live Hosts:** Just knowing a network range isn't enough. You need to determine which IP addresses are actually active and have devices responding on them. This is the most basic step.
- **Discovering Open Ports:** Ports are like doorways into a system. By identifying which ports are open, you can determine which services are running on a host.
- **Service Discovery: Knowing What's Behind the Doors:** Knowing a port is open is only half the story. You need to identify the *service* running on that port (e.g., HTTP, SSH, FTP). This tells you what the system is doing.
- **Operating System Detection: Identifying the Foundation:** Knowing the operating system of a target host can help you identify potential vulnerabilities and tailor your attacks accordingly.
- **Mapping the Network: Seeing the Big Picture:** Network scanning can help you create a map of the entire network, showing the relationships between different devices and services.
- **Inventory:** Understanding the hardware, software, and network equipment on your network.

The Network Scanning Process: A Step-by-Step Approach

Network scanning typically involves the following steps:

1. **Host Discovery:** Identifying active hosts on the network.
2. **Port Scanning:** Identifying open ports on each active host.
3. **Service Detection:** Identifying the services running on each open port.
4. **OS Detection:** Determining the operating system of each host.
5. **Vulnerability scanning:** Identifying known vulnerabilities to services and operating systems found.
6. **Reporting:** Reporting on the state of your network.

We'll explore each of these steps in more detail in the following sections.

Ethical Hacking, Legality, and Responsible Disclosure:

You cannot overstate the importance of this. Before you start scanning any network, you *must* have explicit permission from the owner. Unauthorized network scanning is illegal in most jurisdictions and can have serious consequences. Think of it as trespassing. Ethical hacking is not hacking without permission.

Ethical hackers use their skills to help organizations identify and fix security vulnerabilities *before* malicious actors can exploit them.

Responsible disclosure means reporting vulnerabilities to the vendor or organization in a responsible manner, giving them time to fix the issue before disclosing it publicly.

Ethical Considerations: Walking the Line

Even with permission, ethical considerations are paramount:

- **Scope:** Understand the scope of your engagement. Don't scan outside the agreed-upon boundaries.
- **Impact:** Be aware that network scanning can generate a significant amount of traffic and may impact the performance of the target network. Avoid using aggressive scanning techniques that could disrupt services.
- **Stealth:** Consider using stealth scanning techniques to minimize the risk of detection by intrusion detection systems (IDS). You want to test the real-world security measures, not just trigger alarms.

[I've always been a firm believer in responsible disclosure. When I find a vulnerability, I always report it to the vendor or organization first, giving them a chance to fix it before I disclose it publicly. It's the right thing to do.]

Practical Implication

Imagine you're a newly hired security consultant tasked with assessing the security of a small business network. Your first step would be to perform a network scan to identify all the devices connected to the network, the services they're running, and their operating systems. This information would allow you to prioritize your efforts and focus on the most vulnerable systems.

Or, if you work as a system administrator, you can inventory all the network equipment, software, and versions running.

Scanning Without Scanning

It is also possible to identify resources and vulnerabilities from the outside without scanning. These are referred to as out-of-band methods. A lot of information is available about software and hardware. This knowledge can be leveraged to search for possible network configurations.

Moving Forward: Building Your Skills

Network scanning is a fundamental skill for anyone working in cybersecurity. By understanding the landscape and using the right tools, you can gather valuable information about your target network and identify potential vulnerabilities. As you progress, you'll learn about different scanning techniques, stealth methods, and advanced analysis techniques.

You can create a scanning checklist. You can also organize the information into a network map.

Ready to pick up your first tool? We can start exploring Nmap in the next section.

4.2 Nmap: Host Discovery, Port Scanning, Service Detection: Your Swiss Army Knife for Network Exploration

If network scanning is about exploring the landscape, then Nmap (Network Mapper) is your trusty Swiss Army knife. It's a free and open-source tool that's become the industry standard for network discovery and security auditing. Nmap is incredibly powerful and versatile, allowing you to perform a wide range of scanning techniques, from simple host discovery to in-depth service and OS detection.

Getting Started: Nmap Basics

Before we dive into the details, let's cover the basic syntax for using Nmap:

```
nmap [scan type] [options] target
```

- nmap: The command to run Nmap.
- scan type: Specifies the type of scan to perform (e.g., host discovery, port scanning).
- options: Modifies the behavior of the scan (e.g., specifying the target ports, enabling OS detection).
- target: Specifies the target host or network to scan (e.g., 192.168.1.100, scanme.nmap.org, 192.168.1.0/24).

Nmap requires root privileges. You can run nmap with sudo.

Host Discovery: Finding Active Devices

Host discovery is the process of identifying which IP addresses within a network range are actually in use. It's the first step in any network scan. Nmap offers several different host discovery techniques:

- **-sn (Ping Scan): The Basic Check**

  This option performs a basic ping scan to identify active hosts. It sends ICMP echo requests (ping packets) to the target IP addresses and listens for responses.

  ```
  sudo nmap -sn 192.168.1.0/24
  ```

  This command will send ping packets to all IP addresses in the 192.168.1.0/24 network and display a list of the active hosts.

  Interpreting the Output:

  The output will show you a list of the IP addresses that responded to the ping requests. For example:

  ```
   Nmap scan report for 192.168.1.1
  Host is up (0.0012s latency).
  Nmap scan report for 192.168.1.100
  Host is up (0.0025s latency).
  ```

This indicates that the hosts 192.168.1.1 and 192.168.1.100 are active on the network.

Caveats:

Many firewalls block ICMP traffic, so a ping scan may not always be reliable. If a firewall is blocking ICMP, Nmap may not be able to detect all of the active hosts on the network. There may be more active devices.

- **-PS (TCP SYN Ping): TCP Handshake Check**

  This option sends TCP SYN packets to the target hosts. This is a more reliable host discovery technique than the ping scan, as it is less likely to be blocked by firewalls.

  ```
  sudo nmap -PS22,80,443 192.168.1.0/24
  ```

  This command will send TCP SYN packets to ports 22, 80, and 443 on all IP addresses in the 192.168.1.0/24 network.

  Interpreting the Output:

  The output will show you a list of the IP addresses that responded to the TCP SYN packets.

  Caveats:

  This technique is slightly more intrusive than a ping scan, as it involves sending TCP SYN packets.

- **-PU (UDP Ping): Sending to UDP Ports**

  This option sends UDP packets to the target hosts. This can be useful for discovering hosts that are not responding to TCP SYN packets.

  ```
  sudo nmap -PU53 192.168.1.0/24
  ```

  This command will send UDP packets to port 53 on all IP addresses in the 192.168.1.0/24 network.

This is particularly useful, because DNS typically communicates over port 53 with UDP.

Port Scanning: Identifying Open Doors

Once you've identified the active hosts on a network, the next step is to identify the open ports on each host. This tells you which services are running on the host and which ports are available for communication.

Nmap offers several different port scanning techniques:

- **-sT (TCP Connect Scan): The Full Handshake**

  This option performs a full TCP connection to each target port. It's the most reliable port scanning technique, but it's also the most easily detectable. This is also referred to as a "connect scan".

  ```
  sudo nmap -sT 192.168.1.100
  ```

  This command will attempt to establish a full TCP connection to all ports on the host 192.168.1.100

- **-sS (TCP SYN Scan): The Stealthier Approach**

  This option sends TCP SYN packets to the target ports. If a port is open, the target host will respond with a SYN/ACK packet. This is a more stealthy port scanning technique than the TCP Connect Scan, as it does not complete the full TCP handshake. This is also referred to as a "stealth scan".

  ```
  sudo nmap -sS 192.168.1.100
  ```

  This command will send TCP SYN packets to all ports on the host 192.168.1.100.

  Interpreting the Output:

  The output will show you a list of the open ports on the target host, along with their state (e.g., open, closed, filtered). For example:

  ```
  PORT        STATE    SERVICE
  22/tcp      open       ssh
  ```

```
80/tcp          open       http
443/tcp         open       https
```

This indicates that ports 22, 80, and 443 are open on the host 192.168.1.100.

- **-sU (UDP Scan): Scanning the UDP Landscape**

  This option sends UDP packets to the target ports. UDP scanning can be slower than TCP scanning, as UDP does not guarantee delivery of packets.

  ```
  sudo nmap -sU 192.168.1.100
  ```

  This command will send UDP packets to all ports on the host 192.168.1.100.

- **-p (Port Specification): Narrowing Your Focus**

  This option allows you to specify which ports to scan. You can specify a single port, a range of ports, or a comma-separated list of ports.

  ```
  sudo nmap -p 22,80,443 192.168.1.100
  ```

  This command will scan only ports 22, 80, and 443 on the host 192.168.1.100.

  ```
  sudo nmap -p 1-1000 192.168.1.100
  ```

  This command will scan ports 1 through 1000 on the host 192.168.1.100.

Service Detection: Unmasking the Applications

Knowing that a port is open is useful, but knowing *which* service is running on that port is even more valuable. Service detection allows you to identify the applications and software versions running on the target host.

- **-sV (Version Detection): Probing the Services**

  This option enables version detection. Nmap will connect to the open ports and attempt to identify the service running on each port by sending probes and analyzing the responses.

```
sudo nmap -sV 192.168.1.100
```

This command will perform version detection on all open ports on the host 192.168.1.100.

Interpreting the Output:

The output will show you the service name and version number (if available) for each open port. For example:

```
PORT     STATE    SERVICE      VERSION
22/tcp   open     ssh          OpenSSH 7.6p0 Ubuntu 7ubuntu2
80/tcp   open     http         Apache httpd 2.4.29 ((Ubuntu))
443/tcp  open     ssl/http     Apache httpd 2.4.29 ((Ubuntu))
```

This indicates that the host is running OpenSSH 7.6p0 on port 22, Apache httpd 2.4.29 on port 80, and Apache httpd 2.4.29 over SSL on port 443. The name is listed, as well as the software.

Practical Implication

Imagine you're conducting a penetration test and you discover that a target host is running an outdated version of Apache httpd. You could then use this information to search for known vulnerabilities in that version of Apache and attempt to exploit them.

A Word of Caution:

Network scanning can be noisy and may be detected by intrusion detection systems (IDS). Consider using stealth scanning techniques to minimize the risk of detection. Stealth scanning is described later in the chapter.

Ready to push this more?

4.3 Advanced Nmap Techniques: OS Detection, Version Scanning: Digging Deeper for Hidden Clues

You've mastered the basics of Nmap, learning how to discover hosts, scan ports, and identify services. Now, it's time to unlock Nmap's full potential by exploring advanced techniques like OS detection and version scanning. These techniques allow you to gather even more detailed information about your target, providing valuable insights for both offensive and defensive security measures. Think of these as turning your network scanner into a forensic investigator.

Operating System (OS) Detection: Unmasking the Operating System

Knowing the operating system of a target host is crucial. It allows you to:

- **Identify Potential Vulnerabilities:** Different operating systems have different vulnerabilities. By knowing the OS, you can focus your efforts on exploiting vulnerabilities that are specific to that OS.
- **Tailor Your Attacks:** Different operating systems have different security mechanisms and configurations. By knowing the OS, you can tailor your attacks to bypass these defenses.
- **Understand the System's Role:** The OS can provide clues about the system's role on the network. For example, a Windows Server system is likely to be a domain controller or file server, while a Linux system is more likely to be a web server or database server.
- **-O (Enable OS Detection):**

  To enable OS detection, use the -O option with Nmap.

  ```
  sudo nmap -O 192.168.1.100
  ```

  This command will attempt to determine the operating system of the host 192.168.1.100.

  How It Works:

  Nmap performs OS detection by analyzing the TCP/IP stack fingerprint of the target host. This involves sending a series of specially crafted packets to the host and analyzing the responses. Nmap compares the responses to a database of known OS fingerprints to identify the operating system.

  Interpreting the Output:

  The output of the OS detection scan will show you the operating system that Nmap has identified, along with a confidence level. For example:

  ```
  OS: Linux 3.2 - 4.9
  Device type: general purpose
  Running: Linux 3.X|4.X
  OS details: Linux 3.2 - 4.9
  ```

```
Network Distance: 1 hop
```

This indicates that Nmap has identified the operating system as Linux 3.2 - 4.9 with a high degree of confidence.

Limitations:

OS detection is not always accurate. Nmap relies on fingerprinting techniques, which can be spoofed or modified. Additionally, some operating systems are more difficult to fingerprint than others.

Even if Nmap cannot identify the exact operating system, it can still provide valuable information about the OS family (e.g., Linux, Windows, macOS).

It's important to combine OS detection with other techniques, such as service detection and manual analysis, to get a more complete picture of the target system.

To improve accuracy, it's beneficial to open at least one TCP port and one UDP port.

[Personal Insight Placeholder 1: I've often found that OS detection is more accurate on systems with a variety of open ports and services. The more information Nmap has to work with, the better its chances of identifying the correct OS.]

Practical Examples:

1. **Identify the OS of a web server:**

```
sudo nmap -O <web_server_ip>
```

2. **Identify the OS of a router:**

```
sudo nmap -O <router_ip>
```

Version Scanning: Digging Deeper into Services

Knowing the service running on a port is valuable, but knowing the *version* of that service is even more powerful. Version scanning allows you to identify the specific version of the software running on the target host.

Knowing the version is essential for:

- **Exploiting Known Vulnerabilities:** Many vulnerabilities are specific to certain versions of software. By knowing the version, you can identify potential exploits and target your attacks more effectively.
- **Understanding the Security Posture:** Knowing the version of software can provide insights into the security posture of the system. Outdated versions of software are more likely to have known vulnerabilities and may not have the latest security patches.
- **Gathering Detailed Information:** Version scanning can provide detailed information about the service, such as the product name, version number, and even the build date.
- **-sV (Enable Version Detection):**

To enable version detection, use the -sV option with Nmap.

```
sudo nmap -sV 192.168.1.100
```

This command will attempt to determine the version of the software running on each open port on the host 192.168.1.100.

How It Works:

Nmap performs version scanning by sending probes to the open ports and analyzing the responses. It compares the responses to a database of known service signatures to identify the version of the software.

Interpreting the Output:

The output of the version scan will show you the service name and version number (if available) for each open port. For example:

```
PORT      STATE     SERVICE       VERSION
22/tcp    open      ssh           OpenSSH 7.6p0 Ubuntu 7ubuntu2
80/tcp    open      http          Apache httpd 2.4.29 ((Ubuntu))
443/tcp   open      ssl/http      Apache httpd 2.4.29 ((Ubuntu))
```

This indicates that the host is running OpenSSH 7.6p0 on port 22, Apache httpd 2.4.29 on port 80, and Apache httpd 2.4.29 over SSL on port 443.

Increasing Verbosity:

Using the verbosity options allows for more insight. Using -vvv you can view the Nmap probes that are being used for discovering the service. This allows for understanding *how* the services are found.

Limitations:

Version scanning is not always accurate. Nmap relies on service signatures, which can be outdated or incomplete. Additionally, some services may not provide version information.

It's important to combine version scanning with other techniques, such as OS detection and manual analysis, to get a more complete picture of the target system.

To improve accuracy, use the -A argument in Nmap to use a combination of methods for service detection. The time required for the Nmap scan will increase.

[Personal Insight Placeholder 2: I've often found outdated software versions to be a treasure trove of vulnerabilities. It's one of the first things I look for when conducting a penetration test.]

Practical Examples:

1. **Identify the version of Apache running on a web server:**

```
sudo nmap -sV <web_server_ip>
```

2. **Identify the version of SSH running on a remote server:**

```
sudo nmap -sV <ssh_server_ip> -p 22
```

Script Scanning:

With Nmap it is also possible to use Nmap Scripting Engine (NSE) for finding vulnerabilities. Nmap scripts are written in Lua and can be used to automate various tasks, including vulnerability scanning, exploitation, and reporting.

- To use the script scan, use the --script parameter.

```
sudo nmap --script vuln <host_ip>
```

Aggressive Scan (-A): The All-in-One Approach

For convenience, Nmap provides the -A option, which enables a combination of advanced scanning techniques, including OS detection, version detection, script scanning, and traceroute.

```
sudo nmap -A 192.168.1.100
```

This command will perform an aggressive scan on the host 192.168.1.100, gathering as much information as possible about the target system.

A Word of Caution:

Aggressive scans can be noisy and may be detected by intrusion detection systems (IDS). Use them with caution and only when you have explicit permission from the network owner.

Reporting

Generating reports allows for easier distribution of information. The -o option is used to create Nmap reports.
Three common types exist:

- Normal output (-oN)
- XML output (-oX)
- Grepable output (-oG)

```
sudo nmap -A -oX <host_ip> report.xml
```

In Summary:

OS detection and version scanning are powerful techniques that allow you to gather detailed information about your target systems. By combining these techniques with other Nmap features, you can create a comprehensive picture of the network landscape and identify potential security vulnerabilities. Make sure to consider security restrictions and access.

What comes next?

4.4 Packet Sniffing: Wireshark / tcpdump Basics: Listening to the Network's Secrets

You've learned how to identify hosts, ports, and services on a network. But what if you want to see the actual data being transmitted? That's where packet sniffing comes in. Packet sniffing is the process of capturing and analyzing network traffic, allowing you to "eavesdrop" on the communication between devices.

While the term "eavesdropping" might sound malicious, packet sniffing is an essential skill for network administrators, security professionals, and even ethical hackers. It can be used for:

- **Troubleshooting Network Issues:** Identifying network bottlenecks, diagnosing connectivity problems, and analyzing protocol behavior.
- **Analyzing Network Protocols:** Understanding how different protocols work and identifying potential vulnerabilities.
- **Detecting Malicious Activity:** Identifying unauthorized access, detecting malware infections, and analyzing network attacks.

Important Considerations:

- **Legality:** Packet sniffing is illegal in many jurisdictions without proper authorization. Only sniff traffic on networks that you own or have explicit permission to monitor.
- **Privacy:** Packet sniffing can expose sensitive information, such as passwords, usernames, and credit card numbers. Be careful to handle captured data responsibly and protect the privacy of users.

With that important disclaimer out of the way, let's explore two powerful packet sniffing tools: Wireshark and tcpdump.

Wireshark: The GUI Powerhouse

Wireshark is a free and open-source packet analyzer with a graphical user interface (GUI). It allows you to capture and analyze network traffic in real-time, providing a wealth of information about the packets being transmitted.

- **Capturing Traffic:**

  To start capturing traffic with Wireshark, follow these steps:

1. **Launch Wireshark:** Open Wireshark from your applications menu.
2. **Select an Interface:** Choose the network interface you want to capture traffic on (e.g., eth0, wlan0). If you're unsure, try capturing on all interfaces.
3. **Start Capture:** Click the "Start" button (the blue shark fin icon) to begin capturing traffic.

   Wireshark will now display a live stream of network packets as they are transmitted and received by your system.

You can then select a specific packet and see what it is doing. For example, selecting a packet that used the TCP protocol will allow you to view all the details.

- **Filtering Traffic:**

Wireshark's powerful filtering capabilities allow you to focus on specific traffic of interest. You can filter traffic based on protocol, IP address, port number, and many other criteria.
The filter bar is located at the top of the Wireshark window. To apply a filter, simply type the filter expression into the filter bar and press Enter.

Some common Wireshark filters include:

  - tcp: Show only TCP traffic.
  - udp: Show only UDP traffic.
  - ip.addr == 192.168.1.100: Show only traffic to or from the IP address 192.168.1.100.
  - tcp.port == 80: Show only TCP traffic on port 80 (HTTP).
  - http.request.method == "GET": Show only HTTP GET requests.
  - http.request.uri contains "password": Show only HTTP requests that contain the word "password" in the URI.

If you forget the syntax, click the "Expression..." button to access a menu of expressions and fields that can be used to build filters.

- **Analyzing Packets:**

Wireshark provides a detailed view of each captured packet, showing the different layers of the TCP/IP model and the contents of each layer.

When you select a packet in the main Wireshark window, you'll see three panes:

1. **Packet List Pane (Top):** Displays a list of all captured packets, with summary information such as the source and destination IP addresses, protocol, and packet length.
2. **Packet Details Pane (Middle):** Displays the details of the selected packet, organized by layer (e.g., Ethernet, IP, TCP, HTTP).
3. **Packet Bytes Pane (Bottom):** Displays the raw bytes of the selected packet in hexadecimal and ASCII format.

*Disclaimer: You will need to run Wireshark as a super user, using sudo.

tcpdump: The Command-Line Workhorse

tcpdump is a command-line packet analyzer that allows you to capture and analyze network traffic without a graphical interface. It is a more lightweight alternative to Wireshark and is often used on systems where a GUI is not available or practical.

- **Capturing Traffic:**

  To start capturing traffic with tcpdump, open a terminal and run the following command:

  ```
  sudo tcpdump -i eth0
  ```

  Replace eth0 with the name of the network interface you want to capture traffic on.

  This command will capture all traffic on the eth0 interface and display it in the terminal.

- **Filtering Traffic:**

  tcpdump also supports powerful filtering capabilities. You can filter traffic based on protocol, IP address, port number, and many other criteria.

  Some common tcpdump filters include:

  - tcp: Show only TCP traffic.
  - udp: Show only UDP traffic.

- host 192.168.1.100: Show only traffic to or from the IP address 192.168.1.100.
- port 80: Show only traffic on port 80 (HTTP).
- src port 22: Only from port 22.
- dst port 22: Only to port 22.

You can combine multiple filters using logical operators like and, or, and not.

For example, to show only TCP traffic to or from the IP address 192.168.1.100 on port 80, you would use the following filter:

```
sudo tcpdump -i eth0 tcp and host 192.168.1.100 and port 80
```

- **Saving Traffic to a File:**

  You can save captured traffic to a file for later analysis using the -w option.

```
sudo tcpdump -i eth0 -w capture.pcap
```

This command will save all traffic on the eth0 interface to a file named capture.pcap. You can then open this file in Wireshark for further analysis.

*Disclaimer: You will need to run tcpdump as a super user, using sudo.

Practical Scenarios:

1. **Capture HTTP traffic to analyze web requests:**

```
sudo tcpdump -i eth0 tcp port 80
```

or

```
sudo wireshark
```

Set your filters, and then start capture!

2. **Capture SSH traffic to analyze secure communication:**

```
sudo tcpdump -i eth0 tcp port 22
```

3. **Capture DNS traffic to analyze domain name resolution:**

```
sudo tcpdump -i eth0 udp port 53
```

4. **Capture traffic from or to a specific IP address:**

```
sudo tcpdump -i eth0 host <ip address>
```

1. **Analyze the TCP three-way handshake**:
   - Start a tcpdump capture and look for the SYN, SYN-ACK, and ACK packets. This is the basic of a connection and a required element of network analysis.

In Summary:

Packet sniffing is a powerful technique that allows you to gain deep insights into network communication. By mastering Wireshark and tcpdump, you can become a skilled network detective, able to diagnose network issues, analyze protocols, and detect malicious activity. However, always remember to use these tools responsibly and ethically, respecting the privacy of others and adhering to legal regulations.

Now, let's move on to some out-of-band techniques.

4.5 Passive Reconnaissance: Gathering Intelligence From the Shadows

You've learned how to actively scan a network, but that approach comes with risks. Active scanning can be noisy, generating traffic that alerts the target to your presence. What if you want to gather information *without* directly interacting with the target? That's where passive reconnaissance comes in. Think of it as gathering intelligence by observing from the shadows. It reduces the chances of an attack and helps gather information for a real-world attack.

What is Passive Reconnaissance?

Passive reconnaissance involves gathering information about a target network using publicly available resources, without directly interacting with the target systems.

This is about leveraging existing information rather than probing for it. Passive Reconnaissance includes:

- Search Engines
- Social Media
- WHOIS
- DNS Lookups
- Job Postings
- Code Repositories
- Shodan

Why Use Passive Reconnaissance?

- **Stealth:** Passive reconnaissance is much more difficult to detect than active scanning. You're not sending any traffic to the target network, so there's no risk of triggering intrusion detection systems (IDS).
- **Information Gathering:** It can provide valuable information about the target network, such as the technologies used, the services running, and the security practices in place.
- **Planning and Preparation:** It allows you to plan your attacks more effectively by identifying potential vulnerabilities and attack vectors *before* you even touch the target network. It is also possible, but rare, that vulnerabilities are found at this step.

Common Techniques and Tools:

Let's explore some common passive reconnaissance techniques and the tools you can use to implement them:

- **Search Engines: The Power of Google (and Others)**

  Search engines like Google, DuckDuckGo, and Bing can be powerful tools for gathering information about a target organization. By using advanced search operators, you can find specific information that may not be readily available on the organization's website.

  - **Google Dorking:** Using advanced search operators to find sensitive information.

    Some common Google dorks include:

    - site:target.com: Restricts the search to a specific website.

- filetype:pdf: Searches for PDF documents.
- intitle:"index of": Finds directories that are publicly accessible. This is dangerous, because someone may have left access keys, passwords, and other sensitive information.
- inurl:login: Finds login pages.
- ext:sql | ext:db | ext:mdb: Searches for database files that may contain sensitive information.
- cache:target.com: Display Google's cached version of the webpage. Useful to see old information.

Example:

To find PDF documents on the example.com website, you would use the following search query:

```
site:example.com filetype:pdf
```

- **Social Media: Unveiling Employee Habits and Technologies**

Social media platforms like LinkedIn, Twitter, and Facebook can provide valuable insights into the employees, technologies, and security practices of a target organization.

- **LinkedIn:** Use LinkedIn to identify key personnel within the organization, such as system administrators, security engineers, and developers. You can also find information about their skills, experience, and education.
- **Twitter:** Use Twitter to monitor the organization's online presence and identify any security-related discussions or announcements.
- **Facebook:** Use Facebook to gather information about the organization's culture, values, and employee activities.

Example:

Search for employees of "Example Corp" on LinkedIn to identify system administrators and security engineers:

```
site:linkedin.com "Example Corp" AND "System Administrator"
```

Then, use these employees to search the general web for publicly shared information.

- **WHOIS: Uncovering Ownership and Contact Information**

  WHOIS (Who Is) is a database that contains information about registered domain names and IP addresses. You can use WHOIS to find the contact information for the owner of a domain name or IP address, as well as other information such as the registration date and expiration date.

  To use WHOIS, you can use online WHOIS lookup tools or the whois command-line tool.

```
whois example.com
```

  This command will display the WHOIS information for the example.com domain name.
  You may need to install it with apt.

- **DNS Lookups: Mapping Domain Names to IP Addresses**

  DNS lookups can be used to find the IP addresses associated with a domain name, as well as other information about the domain, such as mail servers and name servers.
  You can use the nslookup or dig commands to perform DNS lookups.

```
nslookup example.com
```

  This command will display the IP address(es) associated with the example.com domain name.

- **Job Postings: Discovering Technologies and Security Practices**

  Job postings can provide valuable insights into the technologies and security practices used by a target organization. By analyzing job descriptions for system administrators, security engineers, and developers, you can get a sense of the skills and technologies that are valued by the organization. You can find which software, anti-virus, equipment they want experience with.

- **Code Repositories: Uncovering Code and Configuration Files**

Code repositories like GitHub, GitLab, and Bitbucket can provide access to source code, configuration files, and other sensitive information about a target organization.

By searching these repositories, you may be able to find:

- API keys
- Passwords
- Database connection strings
- Configuration files

Example:

Search GitHub for files with the .env extension that may contain sensitive environment variables:

```
site:github.com filename:.env
```

- **Shodan: Exploring the Internet of Things**

  Shodan is a search engine that allows you to discover and explore internet-connected devices. Unlike Google, which indexes web pages, Shodan indexes devices such as webcams, routers, servers, and industrial control systems.

  Shodan can be used to identify:

  - Open ports
  - Banner information
  - Vulnerable devices

  Example:

  Search Shodan for webcams with open ports:

  ```
  port:80 webcam
  ```

Putting It All Together: Building a Reconnaissance Profile

The key to effective passive reconnaissance is to combine information from multiple sources to build a comprehensive profile of the target organization.

Start by gathering basic information about the organization, such as its name, website, and physical address. Then, use the techniques described above to gather more detailed information about its employees, technologies, and security practices.

As you gather information, organize it in a structured format, such as a spreadsheet or a mind map. This will help you to identify patterns, connections, and potential vulnerabilities.

You can use your gathered information to create a threat model.

In Summary:

Passive reconnaissance is a powerful technique that allows you to gather valuable information about a target network without directly interacting with it. By mastering these techniques, you can become a skilled intelligence gatherer, able to plan your attacks more effectively and minimize the risk of detection. Just remember that legality is critical and you should be familiar with security regulations when analyzing information. You are ready for the next steps.

Chapter 5: Bash Scripting for Hackers: Automating Your Way to Victory

You've mastered the command line, becoming adept at navigating the file system, analyzing network traffic, and gathering intelligence. Now, it's time to take your skills to the next level by learning how to automate tasks using Bash scripting. Think of this chapter as learning to build your own custom tools and workflows. No longer will you have to do things by hand.

5.1 Introduction to Bash Scripting: Shebang, Execution: Hello, World! (The Hacking Edition)

You've wielded individual commands on the command line, now get ready to amplify your capabilities with the power of Bash scripting. Think of Bash scripts as your custom-built tools, automating repetitive tasks and enabling you to perform complex operations with a single command. For a hacker (ethical or otherwise), scripting is not just useful - it's essential.

Why Bother Scripting? The Hacker's Advantage

Why spend the time writing scripts when you can just type commands directly into the terminal? Because scripting offers several key advantages, especially in the context of hacking and cybersecurity:

- **Automation:** Imagine having to manually run the same series of commands hundreds of times. Scripting allows you to automate these repetitive tasks, saving you time and effort.
- **Efficiency:** Scripts allow you to perform complex operations with a single command. This can be especially useful when dealing with large datasets or complex workflows.
- **Customization:** Scripts allow you to create custom tools and workflows that are tailored to your specific needs. You're no longer limited by the tools that others have created.
- **Reproducibility:** Scripts provide a record of the steps you took to perform a particular task. This makes it easier to reproduce your results and share your techniques with others.
- **Evasion:** Scripts can be used to obfuscate your actions and make it more difficult for defenders to detect your activity.
- **Persistence:** Scripts can be used to maintain persistence on a compromised system, ensuring that you can regain access even after the system is rebooted.

Your First Bash Script: Echoing into the Hacker's Toolkit

Let's create a simple Bash script that prints "Hello, world!" to the console and then displays the current date and time. This will introduce you to the basic syntax and concepts of Bash scripting.

1. **Open a Text Editor:**

   Start by opening a text editor on your Kali Linux system. You can use any text editor you like, such as nano, vim, or gedit. For this example, we'll use nano.

   ```
   nano hello_hacker.sh
   ```

   This command will open the hello_hacker.sh file in the nano text editor. If the file doesn't exist, it will be created.

2. **Add the Shebang Line:**

   The first line of your Bash script should always be the shebang (#!). This tells the system which interpreter to use to execute the script. For Bash scripts, the shebang should be:

   ```
   #!/bin/bash
   ```

   This line tells the system to use the Bash interpreter located at /bin/bash to execute the script.

3. **Write Your Commands:**

   Add the commands you want to execute to the script. For example:

   ```
   #!/bin/bash

   echo "Hello, world! Welcome to the world of Bash scripting
   for hackers."
   date
   ```

   This script will print "Hello, world! Welcome to the world of Bash scripting for hackers." to the console and then display the current date and time.

4. **Save the File:**

   Save the file with a .sh extension (e.g., hello_hacker.sh). The .sh extension is a convention that indicates that the file is a Bash script.

   In nano, press Ctrl+X, then Y, then Enter to save and exit.

5. **Make the Script Executable:**

   Before you can run the script, you need to make it executable. Use the chmod command to change the file permissions:

   ```
   chmod +x hello_hacker.sh
   ```

   This command will add execute permissions to the file for the owner, group, and others.

Understanding File Permissions:

The chmod +x command adds execute permissions to the file. In Linux, file permissions are represented by a series of letters and symbols, such as -rwxr-xr--. The first character indicates the file type (- for a regular file, d for a directory). The next nine characters represent the permissions for the owner, group, and others, respectively.

Each set of three characters represents the read (r), write (w), and execute (x) permissions for the corresponding user category.

By adding the +x option to the chmod command, you are telling the system to grant execute permissions to all users for this file.

6. **Run the Script:**

   Now you can run the script by typing its name in the terminal:

   ```
   ./hello_hacker.sh
   ```

   The ./ prefix tells the system to execute the script from the current directory.

   Important: You must specify the ./ prefix if the current directory is not in your system's PATH environment variable.

Behind the Scenes: How the Shebang Works:

When you execute a script, the operating system uses the shebang line to determine which interpreter to use. The shebang line is a special comment that begins with #! followed by the path to the interpreter.

In the case of #!/bin/bash, the system will use the Bash interpreter located at /bin/bash to execute the script. If the shebang line is missing or incorrect, the system may try to execute the script using a different interpreter, which could lead to unexpected results.

Troubleshooting Common Issues:

- **"Permission Denied" Error:** If you get a "Permission denied" error when trying to run the script, it means the script is not executable. Make sure you have used the chmod +x command to add execute permissions to the file.

- **"Command Not Found" Error:** If you get a "Command not found" error, it means the system cannot find the specified command. Make sure the command is installed on your system and that it is in your system's PATH environment variable.
- **Incorrect Output:** If the script produces incorrect output, check your syntax carefully. Bash is very sensitive to syntax errors, and even a small mistake can cause the script to fail.

Let's use different commands within the bash script. How can we include the user and system information within the bash script?

- The whoami command displays your current username.
- The uname -a command displays all of the system information

Here is an example:

```
#!/bin/bash
echo "Hello, world! Welcome to the world of Bash scripting
for hackers."
echo "Current User: " $(whoami)
echo "System Information: " $(uname -a)
date
```

With that, you are ready for coding to the next level. You can add this file as part of your toolkit or report generator. Do you have any specific topics that I can clarify?

5.2 Variables, Data Types, Operators: Giving Your Scripts the Power to Remember and Calculate

It's time to learn how to store and manipulate data within your scripts. Think of variables as containers for storing information, and operators as the tools for performing calculations and comparisons. These are the building blocks of more complex and powerful scripts.

Variables: Remembering Information

Variables allow you to store data in Bash scripts. You can use variables to store strings, numbers, and other values.

- **Naming Your Variables: A Few Rules to Follow**

Variable names must start with a letter or underscore (_) and can contain letters, numbers, and underscores. Variable names are case-sensitive, meaning that myVariable and myvariable are treated as different variables.

It's a best practice to use descriptive variable names that indicate the purpose of the variable. For example, target_ip is a better variable name than x.

- **Assigning Values: Giving Variables Meaning**

  To assign a value to a variable, use the = operator.

  ```
  target_ip="192.168.1.100"
  ```

  Important: There should be no spaces around the = operator. target_ip = "192.168.1.100" will cause an error.

  You can also assign the output of a command to a variable using command substitution:

  ```
  current_date=$(date)
  ```

  This command will assign the output of the date command to the current_date variable.

- **Accessing Values: Recalling What You Stored**

  To access the value of a variable, use the $ prefix.

  ```
  echo "The target IP address is: $target_ip"
  ```

  This command will print the value of the target_ip variable to the console.

  You can also use curly braces ({}) to explicitly delimit the variable name:

  ```
  echo "The target IP address is: ${target_ip}"
  ```

  This is useful when the variable name is followed by other characters that could be interpreted as part of the variable name.

- **Variable Scope: Where Variables Live**

  The scope of a variable determines where it can be accessed within a script. By default, variables in Bash scripts have global scope, meaning they can be accessed from anywhere in the script.

  You can create local variables using the local keyword. Local variables can only be accessed within the function or block of code in which they are defined.

```
 function my_function {
    local my_local_variable="This is a local variable"
    echo $my_local_variable
}

my_function
echo $my_local_variable  # This will produce an error, as the
variable is out of scope
```

Data Types: What Kind of Data Are You Storing?

Bash is a weakly typed language, which means that you don't need to explicitly declare the data type of a variable. Bash will automatically determine the data type based on the value you assign to the variable.

However, it's important to understand the different data types that Bash supports, as this can affect how you manipulate and process the data.

Common data types in Bash include:

- **String:** A sequence of characters (e.g., "Hello, world!").
- **Number:** An integer or a floating-point number (e.g., 123, 3.14). Note: Bash primarily works with integers. Floating-point arithmetic requires external tools.
- **Array:** A collection of values (e.g., (apple banana cherry)).

Operators: Performing Calculations and Comparisons

Operators are used to perform arithmetic, comparison, and logical operations in Bash scripts.

- **Arithmetic Operators: Crunching Numbers**

- +: Addition
- -: Subtraction
- *: Multiplication
- /: Division
- %: Modulo (remainder)

To perform arithmetic operations, you can use the $(( )) construct.

```
num1=10
num2=5
result=$((num1 + num2))
echo $result   # Output: 15
```

It's important to note that Bash only supports integer arithmetic. If you need to perform floating-point arithmetic, you can use the bc command.

- **Comparison Operators: Making Decisions**

  Comparison operators are used to compare two values. They are typically used in conditional statements.

  - ==: Equal to
  - !=: Not equal to
  - -lt: Less than
  - -gt: Greater than
  - -le: Less than or equal to
  - -ge: Greater than or equal to

```
num1=10
num2=5

if [ $num1 -gt $num2 ]; then
    echo "$num1 is greater than $num2"
else
    echo "$num1 is not greater than $num2"
fi
```

- **Logical Operators: Combining Conditions**

  Logical operators are used to combine multiple conditions.

  - &&: Logical AND (both conditions must be true)

- ||: Logical OR (at least one condition must be true)
- !: Logical NOT (inverts the condition)

```
num1=10
num2=5

if [ $num1 -gt 5 ] && [ $num2 -lt 10 ]; then
    echo "Both conditions are true"
else
    echo "At least one condition is false"
fi
```

I've found that mastering variables and operators is essential for writing scripts that can adapt to different situations and perform complex calculations.]

Example: Building a Dynamic Port Scanner
Create a port scanner that takes a host and port list as input.

```
      #!/bin/bash
target=$1
ports=$2

for port in $(echo $ports | tr "," " "); do
  nc -zv $target $port 2>/dev/null
  if [ $? -eq 0 ]; then
    echo "Port $port is open"
  else
    echo "Port $port is closed"
  fi
done
```

Here's what the code does:

- target=$1: Assigns the first parameter to target variable.
- ports=$2: Assigns the second parameter to ports variable. The parameters are passed when running the bash script. For example: sudo ./portscanner.sh 192.168.1.100 22,80,443.
- for port in $(echo $ports | tr "," " "); do: This loop iterates over each port number in the $ports variable. To make the string 22,80,443 separate into its constituent parts, a translate call is made to change the commas to spaces.
- nc -zv $target $port 2>/dev/null: Using the netcat tool, attempt to make a TCP connection with the given $target and $port. If a connection is established then the port is open. The error messages are suppressed to STDOUT.

- if [$? -eq 0]; then: Checks if the previous command (nc) was successful. $? is a special variable that contains the exit status of the last executed command. A value of 0 typically indicates success, while a non-zero value indicates failure or an error.
  - echo "Port $port is open": If the port is open (i.e., nc command was successful), this line prints a message to the console indicating that the port is open.
  - echo "Port $port is closed": If the port is not open (i.e., nc command failed), this line prints a message indicating that the port is closed.

In Summary:

Variables, data types, and operators are fundamental concepts that allow you to store and manipulate data within your Bash scripts. By mastering these concepts, you can write more complex and powerful scripts that can perform a wide range of tasks. Be sure to familiarize yourself with arithmetic, comparison, and boolean operators for a full repertoire. Remember to watch those types!

5.3 Conditional Statements: if, then, else, elif, fi: Giving Your Scripts the Power to Think

You've learned how to store data and perform calculations in your Bash scripts. Now, it's time to learn how to make decisions based on that data. Conditional statements allow you to execute different blocks of code based on certain conditions. Think of these as giving your scripts the power to "think" and respond to different situations. They are the workhorse for many tests and scripts.

The Power of Choice: Why Conditional Statements Matter

Conditional statements are essential for creating dynamic and flexible scripts that can adapt to different inputs and situations. They allow you to:

- **Validate Input:** Check if user input is valid before processing it.
- **Handle Errors:** Handle errors gracefully by executing different code based on the error condition.
- **Make Decisions:** Make decisions based on the current state of the system, such as the operating system, the network connection, or the presence of certain files.
- **Control Flow:** Control the flow of execution of your script based on certain conditions.

The if Statement: The Foundation of Decision-Making

The if statement is the most basic type of conditional statement. It allows you to execute a block of code if a certain condition is true.

- **Basic Syntax:**

```
if [ condition ]; then
    # Code to execute if condition is true
fi
```

    - if: The keyword that begins the if statement.
    - [condition]: The condition to be evaluated. The [] brackets are used to evaluate the condition.
    - then: The keyword that separates the condition from the code to be executed.
    - # Code to execute if condition is true: The block of code to be executed if the condition is true.
    - fi: The keyword that ends the if statement.
- **Example:**

```
#!/bin/bash

file="myfile.txt"

if [ -f "$file" ]; then
    echo "$file exists"
fi
```

This script checks if the file myfile.txt exists. If it does, it prints a message to the console.

Using Quotes:

It's important to enclose variables in double quotes ("") when using them in conditional statements. This prevents word splitting and ensures that the variable is treated as a single string, even if it contains spaces.

For example, if the variable file contained the value "my file.txt", the [-f $file] test would be interpreted as [-f my file.txt], which would cause an error. By enclosing the variable in double quotes, the test becomes [-f "my file.txt"], which is the correct syntax.

The if-else Statement: Handling Two Possibilities

The if-else statement allows you to execute one block of code if a condition is true and another block of code if the condition is false.

- **Syntax:**

```
if [ condition ]; then
    # Code to execute if condition is true
else
    # Code to execute if condition is false
fi
```

  - else: The keyword that separates the if block from the else block.
  - # Code to execute if condition is false: The block of code to be executed if the condition is false.

- **Example:**

```
#!/bin/bash

file="myfile.txt"

if [ -f "$file" ]; then
    echo "$file exists"
else
    echo "$file does not exist"
fi
```

This script checks if the file myfile.txt exists. If it does, it prints a message to the console indicating that the file exists. Otherwise, it prints a message indicating that the file does not exist.

The if-elif-else Statement: Handling Multiple Conditions

The if-elif-else statement allows you to handle multiple conditions. It allows you to test multiple conditions in sequence and execute a different block of code for each condition.

- **Syntax:**

```
 if [ condition1 ]; then
    # Code to execute if condition1 is true
elif [ condition2 ]; then
```

```
    # Code to execute if condition2 is true
else
    # Code to execute if all conditions are false
fi
```

- elif: The keyword that separates the if block from the elif block.
- [condition2]: The condition to be evaluated in the elif block.
- # Code to execute if condition2 is true: The block of code to be executed if condition2 is true.
- You can have multiple elif blocks in an if-elif-else statement.

- **Example:**

```
#!/bin/bash

num=10

if [ $num -gt 10 ]; then
    echo "$num is greater than 10"
elif [ $num -lt 10 ]; then
    echo "$num is less than 10"
else
    echo "$num is equal to 10"
fi
```

This script checks if the variable num is greater than, less than, or equal to 10. It prints a message to the console indicating the result of the comparison.

Important: Remember that the conditions in the elif statements are only evaluated if the previous conditions are false. The first condition that evaluates to true will be executed, and the rest of the if-elif-else statement will be skipped.

File Test Operators: Checking File Properties

Bash provides several file test operators that can be used to check the properties of files and directories.

- -e: File exists
- -f: File is a regular file
- -d: File is a directory
- -r: File is readable
- -w: File is writable
- -x: File is executable
- -s: File exists and has a size greater than zero

These operators are typically used in conditional statements to check the properties of files before performing operations on them.

Testing strings. You can test strings with the following:

- -z: True if string is null (has zero length).
- -n: True of string is non-null (has length greater than zero).
- string1 == string2 True if the strings are equal.
- string1 != string2 True if the strings are not equal.
- Examples

```
  test -z "$myvar" && echo "Empty" # if it's empty show it
  [[ -n "$myvar" ]] && echo "Not empty" # if not empty, say
so
  [[ "$myvar" == "abc" ]] # if equal, then..
```

Practical Scenarios for Hackers

```
Check if a port is open:
     #!/bin/bash

   1. host=$1
port=$2

   2. nc -zv $host $port 2>/dev/null

   3. if [ $? -eq 0 ]; then
    echo "Port $port is open on $host"
else
   4.  echo "Port $port is closed on $host"
fi
```

This script checks if a given port is open on a given host. It uses the nc command to attempt to establish a TCP connection to the host and port. If the connection is successful, it prints a message indicating that the port is open. Otherwise, it prints a message indicating that the port is closed. The port number has to be a service that is open on the machine.
You can enhance by specifying parameters:

```
#!/bin/bash
# Check if two parameters are specified.
if [ "$#" -ne 2 ]; then
echo "Usage: $0 host port"
exit 1
```

```
fi

host=$1
port=$2

nc -zv $host $port 2>/dev/null

if [ $? -eq 0 ]; then
  echo "Port $port is open on $host"
else
  echo "Port $port is closed on $host"
fi
```

*Example usage: testport.sh 127.0.0.1 80

2. **Check if a file exists before attempting to read it:**

```
      ```bash
#!/bin/bash

file="myfile.txt"

if [ -r "$file" ]; then
    cat "$file"
else
    echo "Error: $file does not exist or is not readable"
fi
```
```

```
This script checks if the file `myfile.txt` exists and is
readable. If it is, it prints the contents of the file to the
console. Otherwise, it prints an error message.
```

1. **Check if a command is installed before attempting to run it:**

```
      #!/bin/bash

    1. command="nmap"

2. if command -v "$command" &> /dev/null
   then
3.   echo "$command is installed"
   else
4.   echo "$command is not installed. Please install it."
   fi
```

The command -v returns back command location. The test is performed. If not installed, instructions can be displayed to install.

I use conditional statements extensively in my Bash scripts to handle different situations and make my scripts more robust. They're an essential tool for any serious scripter.]

Conclusion:

Conditional statements are essential for creating dynamic and flexible Bash scripts that can adapt to different inputs and situations. By mastering the if, then, else, elif, and fi keywords, you can give your scripts the power to "think" and make decisions based on the current state of the system. You can chain logic based on your goals and testing scenarios.

Let's move on. What is next?

5.4 Loops: for, while, until: Unleashing the Power of Repetition

You've mastered the art of decision-making with conditional statements. Now, it's time to learn how to automate repetitive tasks with loops. Think of loops as the engine that drives automation, allowing you to perform the same action on multiple items or until a specific condition is met. They can also be used to enumerate various settings as a form of discovery. For example: listing all files on a file server.

Why Use Loops? Embracing Automation

Loops are essential for creating efficient and powerful Bash scripts that can handle repetitive tasks without requiring manual intervention. This is a huge advantage for:

- **Processing Lists of Files:** Perform the same operation on a list of files, such as renaming, compressing, or analyzing them.
- **Iterating Through IP Addresses:** Scan a range of IP addresses for open ports or vulnerabilities.
- **Monitoring System Resources:** Continuously monitor system resources and take action if certain thresholds are exceeded.
- **Automating Tasks:** Automate complex workflows that involve multiple steps.

The for Loop: Iterating Over a Collection

The for loop is used to iterate over a list of items, executing a block of code for each item in the list. It is great for doing tasks that are known.

- **Basic Syntax:**

```
        for variable in item1 item2 item3 ...
do
    # Code to execute for each item
done
```

    - for: The keyword that begins the for loop.
    - variable: The name of the variable that will hold the current item in the list.
    - in: The keyword that separates the variable name from the list of items.
    - item1 item2 item3 ...: The list of items to iterate over.
    - do: The keyword that begins the block of code to be executed.
    - # Code to execute for each item: The block of code to be executed for each item in the list.
    - done: The keyword that ends the for loop.
- **Example:**

```
        #!/bin/bash

for file in *.txt
do
    echo "Processing file: $file"
    # Add code to process the file here
done
```

This script iterates over all files with the .txt extension in the current directory and prints their names to the console. You can use any other commands after and during processing of the file.

- **Iterating over a command:**

The for loop can also be used to iterate over the output of a command:

```
#!/bin/bash
# Lists all users on a machine
for user in $(cut -d: -f1 /etc/passwd)
do
echo "User: $user"
done
```

Cut out the first column using delimiter : from the etc/passwd file and print it. The command lists all the users on a linux machine. You can then use this as part of the script to manage users.

Remember: The items in the list can be strings, numbers, or even the output of another command.

- **Number Ranges using Braces:**

Bash provides a convenient way to generate sequences of numbers using braces.

Example:

```
#!/bin/bash

for i in {1..5}; do
 echo Number: $i
done
```

[Personal Insight Placeholder 1: I use for loops constantly to automate tasks that involve processing multiple files or iterating over a list of IP addresses. It's a huge time-saver.]

The while Loop: Repeating Until a Condition is Met

The while loop executes a block of code as long as a certain condition is true. It is great for doing tasks while an input is being streamed.

- **Basic Syntax:**

```
 while [ condition ]
do
    # Code to execute while condition is true
done
```

  - while: The keyword that begins the while loop.
  - [condition]: The condition to be evaluated.
  - do: The keyword that begins the block of code to be executed.
  - # Code to execute while condition is true: The block of code to be executed as long as the condition is true.
  - done: The keyword that ends the while loop.
- **Example:**

```
#!/bin/bash

count=1

while [ $count -le 5 ]
do
    echo "Count: $count"
    count=$((count + 1))
done
```

This script initializes a variable count to 1 and then executes a loop that prints the value of count and increments it by 1 as long as count is less than or equal to 5.

Common Pitfall: Make sure the condition in the while loop eventually becomes false. Otherwise, the loop will run indefinitely, creating an infinite loop.

The until Loop: Repeating Until a Condition is True

The until loop executes a block of code until a certain condition is true. It is the opposite of the while loop. The until loop can help do a test every N seconds.

- **Basic Syntax:**

```
until [ condition ]
do
    # Code to execute until condition is true
done
```

  - until: The keyword that begins the until loop.
  - [condition]: The condition to be evaluated.
  - do: The keyword that begins the block of code to be executed.
  - # Code to execute until condition is true: The block of code to be executed until the condition is true.
  - done: The keyword that ends the until loop.
- **Example:**

```
#!/bin/bash

count=1

until [ $count -gt 5 ]
do
    echo "Count: $count"
```

```
    count=$((count + 1))
done
```

This script initializes a variable count to 1 and then executes a loop that prints the value of count and increments it by 1 until count is greater than 5.

Controlling the Loop: break and continue

Bash provides two keywords for controlling the execution of loops:

- break: Terminates the loop immediately and transfers control to the statement following the loop.
- continue: Skips the current iteration of the loop and continues with the next iteration.

Practical Scenarios: Automating Hacking Tasks

1. **Port Scanning a List of Hosts:**
   To enhance the previous port scanner, it would be useful to have a script scan multiple hosts.

```
 #!/bin/bash
if [ "$#" -lt 2 ]; then
echo "Usage: $0 host1,host2,... port1,port2,..."
exit 1
fi
hosts=$1
ports=$2

for host in $(echo $hosts | tr "," " "); do
echo "Beginning scan of $host"
for port in $(echo $ports | tr "," " "); do
 nc -zv $host $port 2>/dev/null
  if [ $? -eq 0 ]; then
    echo "Port $port is open"
  else
    echo "Port $port is closed"
  fi
done
echo "Finished scan of $host"
done
```

*Example usage: ./multiscan.sh 127.0.0.1,192.168.1.100 22,80,443
This allows you to scan multiple machines at the same time!
2. **Monitor System Resources:**

```
 ```bash
#!/bin/bash

while true
do
    cpu_usage=$(top -bn1 | grep "Cpu(s)" | sed "s/.*id: \([0-9.]*\).*/\1/" | awk '{print 100 - $1}')
    memory_usage=$(free -m | awk 'NR==2{printf "%.2f%%\n", $3*100/$2 }')

    echo "CPU Usage: $cpu_usage%"
    echo "Memory Usage: $memory_usage%"

    sleep 5
done
```

```
This script continuously monitors the CPU and memory usage of the system and prints the results to the console every 5 seconds.

Caveats: This is a very intrusive test and may affect the results.
```

1. **Log Analysis:**

```
#!/bin/bash
# Specify the log file and search pattern
log_file="/var/log/auth.log"
search_pattern="Failed password"

# Loop through the log file and search for the pattern
while IFS= read -r line; do
  if [[ $line == *$search_pattern* ]]; then
    echo "Found suspicious activity:"
    echo "$line"
  fi
done < "$log_file"
```

The combination of loops and conditional statements allows you to create incredibly powerful and flexible Bash scripts that can automate almost any task. It's a skill that every hacker should master.]

In Summary:
```

Loops are fundamental for automating repetitive tasks and creating efficient Bash scripts. By mastering the for, while, and until keywords, along with the break and continue statements, you can write scripts that can handle complex workflows and adapt to different situations. These help reduce manual effort and free up time for other tasks. You are well on your way. What to do next?

5.5 Functions: Creating Reusable Code: Building Blocks for Scripting Mastery

You've learned how to use loops and conditional statements to create more complex Bash scripts. Now, it's time to learn how to organize your code into reusable blocks using functions. Think of functions as the LEGO bricks of scripting, allowing you to build complex structures from smaller, well-defined components. This allows for easier to use code as a standard building block.

Why Use Functions? The Power of Modularity

Functions are essential for creating maintainable and scalable Bash scripts. They allow you to:

- **Organize Your Code:** Break down your script into smaller, more manageable pieces.
- **Reuse Code:** Define a function once and then call it multiple times from different parts of your script.
- **Improve Readability:** Make your code easier to read and understand by giving meaningful names to your functions.
- **Reduce Redundancy:** Eliminate duplicated code, making your scripts more concise and efficient.
- **Enhance Maintainability:** Make it easier to modify and update your scripts by isolating changes to specific functions.

Defining a Function: Giving Your Code a Name

To define a function in Bash, use the function keyword followed by the function name and a pair of parentheses. The code to be executed by the function is enclosed in curly braces {}.

- **Basic Syntax:**

```
  function function_name {
# Code to execute
```

```
}
```

Alternatively, you can omit the function keyword:

```
    function_name() {
  # Code to execute
}
```

- function: The keyword that begins the function definition (optional).
- function_name: The name of the function.
- (): Parentheses that follow the function name.
- {}: Curly braces that enclose the code to be executed by the function.
- # Code to execute: The block of code to be executed when the function is called.

- **Example:**

```
    function greet {
  echo "Hello, world!"
}
```

This defines a function called greet that prints "Hello, world!" to the console.

Calling a Function: Putting Your Code to Work

To call a function, simply type its name in the script.
You can only call it after you define it.

```
greet
```

This will execute the code within the greet function, printing "Hello, world!" to the console.

Passing Arguments to a Function: Making Your Functions Dynamic

You can pass arguments to a function by specifying them after the function name when you call it. Inside the function, you can access the arguments using the $1, $2, $3, etc. variables. You can access all arguments with $@ and $# will give you a count of the number of arguments.

- **Example:**

```
function greet {
   echo "Hello, $1!"
}

greet "John"  # Output: Hello, John!
greet "Jane"  # Output: Hello, Jane!
```

This defines a function called greet that takes one argument (a name) and prints a personalized greeting to the console.
Example with multiple inputs and all inputs.

```
     function multi_greet {
    echo "Hello, first $1 and second $2!"
    echo "All parameters: $@"
    echo "Number of parameters: $#"
}

multi_greet "John" "Jane" # Output: Hello, first John and
second Jane!
#Output:  All parameters: John Jane
#Output:  Number of parameters: 2
```

Returning Values from a Function: Getting Results Back

Functions can return values using the `return` keyword. The return value must be an integer between 0 and 255. This return value is the exit status of the function, which can be accessed using the `$?` variable.

If you want to return a string or other type of data from a function, you can use `echo` and capture the output using command substitution.

*   **Example: Returning a String:**

```bash
function get_username {
    username=$(whoami)
    echo "$username"
}

current_user=$(get_username)
echo "Current user: $current_user"
```

This defines a function called `get_username` that returns the current username. The output of the `whoami` command is captured and echoed from the function. The `current_user` variable is then assigned the output of the `get_username` function.

*   **Returning an Integer (Exit Status):**

```bash
function check_file {
    file="$1"
    if [ -f "$file" ]; then
        echo "$file exists"
        return 0  # Success
    else
        echo "$file does not exist"
        return 1  # Failure
    fi
}

check_file "myfile.txt"
if [ $? -eq 0 ]; then
    echo "File check successful"
else
    echo "File check failed"
fi
```

Important: Returning values from functions can be a bit tricky in Bash. Remember that the `return` keyword only returns an integer exit status. If you want to return other types of data, you'll need to use `echo` and command substitution.

[Personal Insight Placeholder 1: I often use functions to create reusable code blocks for common tasks, such as parsing log files, validating user input, or performing network scans. It makes my scripts much easier to maintain and extend.]

Practical Examples: Building a Reusable Toolkit

1. **Function to Check if a Command is Installed:**

```bash
function is_command_installed {
    command -v "$1" >/dev/null 2>&1
}

if is_command_installed "nmap"; then
    echo "Nmap is installed"
else
    echo "Nmap is not installed"
fi
```

```

This defines a function called `is_command_installed` that checks if a given command is installed on the system. It returns 0 if the command is installed and 1 if it is not.

2. **Function to Validate an IP Address:**

```bash
function validate_ip() {
local ip=$1
local regex="^([0-9]{1,3}\.){3}[0-9]{1,3}$"
if [[ $ip =~ $regex ]]; then
 echo "Valid IP address"
 return 0
else
 echo "Invalid IP address"
 return 1
fi
}
```

Example Test

```
validate_ip 192.168.1.100
echo $?  # Output 0 or 1
validate_ip 999.999.999.999
echo $? # Output 0 or 1
```

In Summary:

Functions are essential for creating modular, maintainable, and reusable Bash scripts. By mastering the techniques of defining, calling, and passing arguments to functions, you can build a powerful toolkit of reusable code blocks that can be used in a wide range of scripting scenarios. This helps reduce effort and speeds up tasks. What comes next?

Chapter 6: Automating Hacking Tasks with Scripts: Putting Your Skills to Work

You've built a solid foundation in Bash scripting, learning how to store data, make decisions, repeat actions, and create reusable code blocks. Now, it's time to put your skills to work by automating common hacking tasks. Think of this chapter as
```

learning how to build your own custom tools for penetration testing, security auditing, and other cybersecurity activities.

Disclaimer: Remember to use these skills ethically and legally. Only automate tasks on systems that you own or have explicit permission to test.

6.1 Scripting for Network Scanning: Building Your Own Reconnaissance Tool

Network scanning is a fundamental task for any hacker, but it can be time-consuming if done manually. By automating network scanning with Bash scripts, you can quickly and efficiently gather information about your target network.

- **Basic Network Scanner:**

  Let's create a simple Bash script that performs a ping scan on a given network range and displays the active hosts.

```
#!/bin/bash

# Set the network to scan
network=$1

# Check if a network is specified
if [ -z "$network" ]; then
    echo "Usage: $0 <network>"
    exit 1
fi

# Perform host discovery
echo "Performing host discovery on $network..."
for ip in $(seq 1 254); do
    ping -c 1 $network.$ip > /dev/null 2>&1
    if [ $? -eq 0 ]; then
        echo "$network.$ip is up"
    fi
done

echo "Host discovery complete."
```

  This script takes a network range as input (e.g., 192.168.1) and then iterates through all IP addresses in that range (1-254). For each IP address, it performs a ping test and displays a message if the host is up.

Modifications:

- Logging: To improve, the script can be modified to log the ping results into a file

- **Port Scanner:**

Let's create a simple Bash script that performs a TCP connect scan on a given host and displays the open ports.

```
#!/bin/bash

# Set the target host
host=$1

# Set the port range
port_start=1
port_end=100

# Check if a host is specified
if [ -z "$host" ]; then
    echo "Usage: $0 <host>"
    exit 1
fi

# Perform port scanning
echo "Performing TCP connect scan on $host..."
for port in $(seq $port_start $port_end); do
    nc -zv $host $port > /dev/null 2>&1
    if [ $? -eq 0 ]; then
        echo "Port $port is open"
    fi
done

echo "Port scanning complete."
```

This script takes a host as input (e.g., 192.168.1.100) and then iterates through a range of ports (1-100). For each port, it attempts to establish a TCP connection using nc (netcat). If the connection is successful, it prints a message indicating that the port is open.

[Personal Insight Placeholder 1: These basic scripts are a great starting point for automating network scanning. You can then customize them to perform more advanced techniques, such as service detection, OS detection, and vulnerability scanning.]

6.2 Scripting for Password Cracking (Dictionary Attacks): Automating the Guessing Game

Password cracking is a topic that requires a *very* serious disclaimer. This section is intended for educational purposes only. Performing password cracking without explicit authorization is illegal and unethical. The following examples should only be used on systems that you own or have explicit permission to test. This topic can be used to check the password strength of various machines and to create stronger safeguards to protect systems.

With that said, understanding how password cracking works is crucial for any security professional or ethical hacker. It allows you to:

- **Assess Password Strength:** Evaluate the strength of passwords used on your systems.
- **Identify Weak Accounts:** Find accounts with weak or default passwords that are vulnerable to attack.
- **Improve Security Practices:** Implement stronger password policies and educate users about the importance of strong passwords.

In this section, we'll focus on automating dictionary attacks, which is one of the most common password cracking techniques.

What is a Dictionary Attack?

A dictionary attack involves trying a list of common passwords against the target account. The list of passwords, known as a dictionary, can be a simple text file containing common words, phrases, and names.

The Script: Automating the Password Guessing

Let's create a simple Bash script that performs a dictionary attack against an SSH server.

```
#!/bin/bash

# Set the target host and username
host=$1
username=$2
wordlist=$3

# Check if the required arguments are specified
```

```
if [ -z "$host" ] || [ -z "$username" ] || [ -z "$wordlist"
]; then
    echo "Usage: $0 <host> <username> <wordlist>"
    exit 1
fi

# Perform dictionary attack
echo "Performing dictionary attack against
$username@$host..."
while read password
do
    sshpass -p "$password" ssh -o StrictHostKeyChecking=no
$username@$host "echo Success"
    if [ $? -eq 0 ]; then
        echo "Password cracked: $password"
        exit 0
    fi
done < "$wordlist"

echo "Password cracking failed."
exit 1
```

This script takes a host, a username, and a wordlist as input. It then iterates through each password in the wordlist and attempts to log in to the SSH server using that password. If the login is successful, it prints a message indicating that the password has been cracked and exits.

Understanding the Script:

- host=$1, username=$2, wordlist=$3: Assigns the command-line arguments to variables.
- if [-z "$host"] || [-z "$username"] || [-z "$wordlist"]; then: Checks if all required arguments are provided.
- sshpass -p "$password" ssh -o StrictHostKeyChecking=no $username@$host "echo Success": Attempts to log in to the SSH server using the current password. The sshpass command is used to provide the password to the ssh command. The -o StrictHostKeyChecking=no option is used to suppress the warning message that is generated when the script connects to a new SSH server.
- if [$? -eq 0]; then: Checks if the login was successful. If it was, the script prints a message indicating that the password has been cracked and exits.
- done < "$wordlist": Reads each line from the wordlist and assigns it to the password variable.

  To make the script more robust, the connection should check the username and password and exit if they exist. In real-world scenarios, these would be unique.

Ethical Considerations:

This example is intended for educational purposes only. Performing password cracking without explicit authorization is illegal and unethical.

- **Use Strong Passwords:** Encourage users to choose strong and unique passwords to protect their accounts.
- **Implement Account Lockout Policies:** Implement account lockout policies to prevent attackers from trying too many passwords in a short period of time.
- **Use Multi-Factor Authentication:** Enable multi-factor authentication (MFA) to add an extra layer of security to your accounts.
- **Monitor for Suspicious Activity:** Monitor your systems for suspicious activity, such as failed login attempts.
- **Comply With All Applicable Laws and Regulations:** Performing any tests can get you arrested if you do not receive the proper approvals.

Using the Script:

1. This requires sshpass
   First, you may need to use to use apt to install the tool.
2. To test the program, setup a local VM for penetration tests.

Enhancing the Dictionary Attack:

1. **Using Different Passwords:** There are many well known password text files that can be found on the internet. There is no single "best" set of passwords, and each set has different tradeoffs.
2. **Parallel Processing:** The script can be modified to use parallel processing to speed up the attack. This involves running multiple instances of the sshpass command simultaneously, allowing you to try more passwords in a shorter period of time.
3. **Logging:** The script can be modified to log the results of the attack to a file. This can be useful for tracking progress and analyzing the effectiveness of the attack.

[Personal Insight Placeholder 1: I've seen firsthand the devastating consequences of weak passwords. It's essential to educate users about the importance of strong

passwords and implement security measures to protect against password cracking attacks.]

Limitations of Dictionary Attacks:

Dictionary attacks are effective against weak passwords, but they are less effective against strong passwords that are not in the dictionary.

To crack stronger passwords, you may need to use more advanced techniques, such as:

- **Brute-Force Attacks:** Trying every possible combination of characters.
- **Rainbow Table Attacks:** Using precomputed tables of password hashes.
- **Social Engineering:** Tricking users into revealing their passwords.

These techniques are more complex and require more resources, but they can be effective against even the strongest passwords. As the saying goes, every system is hackable, provided enough time and money.

In Summary:

Password cracking is a powerful technique that can be used to assess the security of your systems and identify weak accounts. It is best to focus on systems on the network to test, as you may not be able to access the actual hashes for the accounts. But this knowledge must be used ethically and legally. Remember to use these skills to protect your systems, not to attack them. As always, be aware of security regulations and be on the lookout for new attack patterns to make the world a little bit more secure.
What comes next?

6.3 Log Analysis & Event Detection Scripts: Finding Needles in Haystacks of Data

In today's complex and dynamic IT environments, log files are a treasure trove of information. They contain a record of system activity, security events, and potential attacks. However, manually sifting through these log files can be a tedious and time-consuming task. That's where log analysis and event detection scripts come in. Think of these scripts as your automated security analysts, constantly monitoring your logs for suspicious activity and alerting you to potential threats.

Why Automate Log Analysis? The Power of Proactive Security

Automated log analysis offers several key advantages:

- **Real-Time Monitoring:** Scripts can continuously monitor log files for suspicious activity in real-time, allowing you to respond to security incidents more quickly.
- **Early Threat Detection:** By identifying patterns and anomalies in the logs, you can detect potential threats before they cause significant damage.
- **Improved Security Posture:** Log analysis can help you identify weaknesses in your security configuration and improve your overall security posture.
- **Compliance:** Many regulatory compliance frameworks require organizations to monitor and analyze their logs for security events.
- **Efficiency:** Scripts automate the task and reduce the need to do it manually.

Essential Tools: grep, awk, sed, and More

Before we start building our log analysis scripts, let's review some essential commands that you'll need:

- **grep:** Searches for lines in a file that match a specific pattern. This is the foundation of many log analysis scripts.
- grep -i - case insensitive
- grep -r - recursive

```
grep "error" /var/log/syslog
```

- **awk:** A powerful tool for processing text files. It allows you to extract specific fields, perform calculations, and format the output.

```
#Print the fifth and first column
awk '{print $5, $1}' /var/log/apache2/access.log
```

- **sed:** A stream editor that can be used to perform text transformations. This script can search through the log files, extract data, substitute with existing text, and perform other useful transformations.

```
sed 's/search/replace/g' /var/log/apache2/access.log
```

- **cut:** Used for extracting columns.

```
cut -d ',' -f 1,3 data.csv
```

- **sort:** Used to sort the data for easier reading

```
sort access.log
```

- **uniq:** Used for identifying duplicate entries.
-

```
sort access.log | uniq -c
```

- **date:** Used for time ranges and to list log files by time.

  These tools can be piped together in a single script to extract key information.
  For example:

```
grep "error" /var/log/syslog | awk '{print $1, $2, $3}'
| sort | uniq -c
```

I've found that combining these tools in creative ways can allow you to extract incredibly valuable insights from your log files.

Building the Analysis:

1. **Keyword Search:**

   Let's start with a simple Bash script that analyzes a log file for specific keywords and displays the matching lines.

```
#!/bin/bash

# Set the log file and search pattern
log_file=$1
search_pattern=$2

# Check if the required arguments are specified
if [ -z "$log_file" ] || [ -z "$search_pattern" ]; then
    echo "Usage: $0 <log_file> <search_pattern>"
    exit 1
fi
```

```
# Analyze the log file
echo "Analyzing log file $log_file for pattern
'$search_pattern'..."
grep "$search_pattern" "$log_file"

echo "Log analysis complete."
```

The script uses if [-z "$log_file"] to confirm input. There is no check on the ability to read the file. Consider whether you want to confirm file read permissions or check

This script takes a log file and a search pattern as input. It then uses the `grep` command to search for lines in the log file that contain the search pattern and displays the matching lines to the console.

1. **Failed Login Attempts:**

   Let's create a script that identifies failed login attempts in the system authentication log (/var/log/auth.log).

```
#!/bin/bash

# Set the log file and search pattern
log_file="/var/log/auth.log"
search_pattern="Failed password"

# Analyze the log file
echo "Analyzing log file $log_file for failed login
attempts..."
grep "$search_pattern" "$log_file" | awk '{print $1, $2, $3,
$9, $10}'

echo "Log analysis complete."
```

   This script searches for lines in the /var/log/auth.log file that contain the string "Failed password". It then uses the awk command to extract the date, time, and username from the matching lines. We can add these steps to check for potential login attempts:

   It would also be advantageous to find common source IP addresses that are performing this operation.

2. **Unique IP Addresses:**

Find the unique source IP addresses used to conduct the scan.

```
        #!/bin/bash

# Set the log file and search pattern
log_file=$1
search_pattern=$2

# Check if the required arguments are specified
if [ -z "$log_file" ] || [ -z "$search_pattern" ]; then
        echo "Usage: $0 <log_file> <search_pattern>"
        exit 1
fi

# Analyze the log file
echo "Analyzing log file $log_file for failed login
attempts..."
grep "$search_pattern" "$log_file" | awk '{print $(NF-5)}' |
sort | uniq -c
echo "Unique list of IP addresses"
echo "Log analysis complete."
exit 0
```

This uses awk to find the unique values for IP addresses. Then these addresses are compared and listed. The addresses from the commands can then be extracted and saved. These are then extracted, sorted, then the unique values are counted.
You are then ready for the next step.

`Note: These logs may have a lot of personal data and are stored with elevated permissions. Be cautious of the data that you are accessing!`

6. Combining multiple logs
```bash
#!/bin/bash

List of log files to analyze

```
log_files=("/var/log/auth.log" "/var/log/syslog")
```

Search pattern

```
search_pattern="error"
```

Loop through each log file
```

for log_file in "

```
logfiles[@]";doif[-e"{log_files[@]}"; do
      if [ -e "logfiles[@]";doif[-e"

log_file" ]; then
echo "Analyzing
              logfilefor'log_file for 'logfilefor'

      search_pattern':"
      grep "
              searchpattern""search_pattern" "searchpattern""

      log_file" || echo "No matches found"
      else
      echo "$log_file does not exist."
      fi
      done
```

The script uses `if [ -e "$log_file" ]; then` to confirm file exists. There is no check on the ability to read the file. Consider whether you want to confirm file read permissions or check. Also, you may need to include `sudo` for elevated permissions or the script might fail to work

This allows the review of multiple key logs at one time. *[Personal Insight Placeholder 2: Log analysis can be a powerful tool for detecting security incidents and identifying potential vulnerabilities. It's essential to have a system in place to monitor and analyze your logs on a regular basis.]*

Key Practices for Effective Log Analysis:

* **Define Clear Objectives:** Before you start analyzing your logs, define your objectives. What are you looking for? What kind of events are you interested in detecting?
* **Use Specific Search Patterns:** The more specific your search patterns, the more accurate and efficient your log analysis will be.
* **Automate the Process:** Automate your log analysis scripts to run on a regular basis. This will help you to detect security incidents in real-time. You can use cron jobs to schedule your scripts to run automatically.

In Summary:

Log analysis is a critical task for any security professional or system administrator. By automating log analysis with Bash scripts, you can quickly and efficiently identify suspicious activity and respond to security incidents more effectively. Understanding the right tools and commands will provide valuable insights. In what other ways can we connect these scripts?

6.4 Automating Repetitive Tasks: Tying It All Together- Building Your Custom Workflow

You've now acquired the essential skills to build your own tools. From setting up a computer to password cracking to intrusion detection, it is time to create a script that runs the process from the beginning.
This chapter will focus on putting together a script that will:

- Update system and network settings
- Run basic tools
- Report on the status of those tools

Let's create a script that runs the process from the beginning:

Creating an Automated Network Scanner

Let's say you want a script to scan and make persistent file changes.
It is beneficial to include the following:

- The IP or host to scan as the parameter
- Ability to modify persistent files (and confirmation steps)
- Have functions for common actions

```
    #!/bin/bash

# Script to perform various maintenance tasks

# Function to check for root privileges
check_root() {
    if [[ $EUID -ne 0 ]]; then
        echo "This script must be run as root."
        exit 1
    fi
}

# Function to update the system
update_system() {
    echo "Updating the system..."
    apt update && apt upgrade -y
}

# Function to scan a host
scan_host() {
```

```
        local host=$1
        echo "Scanning host: $host"
        nmap -T4 -A -v $host
}

#Main program
check_root
update_system

if [ -n "$1" ]; then
  scan_host $1
else
  echo "Please specify host to scan."
  exit 1
fi

echo "Finished"
exit 0
```

Here is a breakdown:

- **check_root()**: The script confirms you are using sudo.
- **update_system()**: The script runs apt update && apt upgrade -y
- **scan_host()**: The script uses Nmap with parameters -T4 -A -v against a given IP.

What does this do? This will perform a general scan of the top 1000 most common ports on the host and get a good picture of running services.
You may want to include log-rotate, but Nmap can have elevated disk space usage.

[Personal Insight Placeholder 1: Often the most important part of a system is confirming access to the correct log files. Checking permissions, security settings, and other variables, such as those described in this chapter, can help automate the task and ensure correct implementation.]

Customizing
To further enhance the scripts, the existing script can be modified by adding or removing steps.

- Replace "google.com" with a variable representing a specific hostname or IP address.
- Modify the type of test to the address, based on ping, DNS, port 80, and/or a particular flag.
  The command can run all automatically or wait on confirmation.

Disclaimer: All security checks and tests require you to be granted permission by the network operator.

What about password complexity settings or disk encryption?
Those tests will be a little trickier and will require more steps.

Handling Output/Reporting
After everything is done, it is also possible to print out a report or log output.
Let's create a script that runs and generates a report.
Create a file called scriptedports.sh that will contain the script
Edit the script to contain the following information:

```
      #!/bin/bash
# Testing specific ports.
ports=(21 22 80 443 3389)
# Setting the values for tests
 TIMEFORMAT=%R

echo "Starting the test!"

if [ -z $1 ]; then
        echo "Usage: $0 <target>"
        exit 1
fi
target=$1

 if  ! (ping -c 1 $target &> /dev/null)
 then
        echo "Ping failed. Check network!"
  exit 1
 fi

echo "Pinging: " $target " was successful! Now proceeding.."

for port in ${ports[@]}; do
echo "Checking port:" $port
if ! (nc -zvn $target $port) then
        echo "Port" $port " is closed."
 else
        echo "Port" $port " is open."
 fi
done

echo "Finished!"
exit 0
```

- To set the values for ports that will be tested, the ports are given to the Ports variable as an array. If more ports are wanted, then it is just a matter of adding them to the line separated by spaces.
- An initial check is used with Ping to see if there is an available computer with the specified IP. If the test does not reach the IP, then the script will exit. If it does, then it will move onto the port tests.
- As the script checks port status, it will list whether the port is open or closed.

This script automates most of the key aspects of securing a system. It can be modified for additional steps and processes.
Key Takeaways

- **Break Down Tasks:** Identify repetitive tasks that can be automated with scripts.
- **Start Simple:** Begin with small, simple scripts and gradually add more complexity.
- **Use Functions:** Organize your code into reusable functions to improve readability and maintainability.
- **Test Thoroughly:** Test your scripts thoroughly to ensure that they work as expected and do not introduce any new vulnerabilities.
- **Document Your Code:** Add comments to your code to explain what it does and why. This will make it easier to understand and maintain your scripts in the future.
  Do you wish to do a deeper analysis of what is needed in network enumeration and testing for systems?

Chapter 7: Basic Exploitation Concepts: Understanding the Attacker's Mindset

Now that you've learned how to scan networks and gather information, it's time to delve into the world of exploitation. This chapter is not about teaching you how to become a malicious hacker. Instead, it's about understanding the *attacker's mindset* and learning how vulnerabilities can be exploited so that you can better protect your systems.

Disclaimer: It is crucial to understand that exploitation should only be performed on systems that you own or have explicit permission to test. Unauthorized exploitation is illegal and unethical.

7.1 Introduction to Vulnerabilities and Exploits: Seeing the World Through an Attacker's Eyes (Ethically!)

Before you can defend a system, you need to understand how attackers think. This section introduces the core concepts of vulnerabilities and exploits, laying the groundwork for understanding how attackers can compromise systems and what you can do to prevent it. Remember, this knowledge is to protect, not to destroy!

What is a Vulnerability? The Chink in the Armor

A vulnerability is a weakness or flaw in a system's design, implementation, or configuration that can be exploited by an attacker to gain unauthorized access, cause damage, or disrupt service. Think of it as a chink in the armor, a gap in the defenses that an attacker can use to their advantage.

Vulnerabilities can exist in various parts of a system:

- **Software:** Bugs in code, such as buffer overflows, SQL injection flaws, or cross-site scripting (XSS) vulnerabilities.
- **Hardware:** Design flaws or manufacturing defects that can be exploited.
- **Network Configuration:** Misconfigured firewalls, weak access controls, or insecure protocols.
- **Human Factor:** Weak passwords, social engineering susceptibility, or lack of security awareness.

What is an Exploit? The Key to Unlocking the Vulnerability

An exploit is a piece of code, a technique, or a sequence of actions that takes advantage of a vulnerability to achieve a specific goal. Think of it as the key that unlocks the vulnerability, allowing the attacker to achieve their objective.

An exploit isn't always a single, self-contained program. It can be a combination of actions, commands, and data that, when executed in a specific order, trigger the vulnerability and achieve the desired outcome.

The Vulnerability → Exploit → Payload Chain: A Step-by-Step Breakdown

Often, the exploitation process involves a chain of events:

1. **Vulnerability:** The initial weakness or flaw in the system.
2. **Exploit:** The method used to trigger or take advantage of the vulnerability.

3. **Payload:** The malicious code that is delivered by the exploit and executed on the target system.

The payload is the attacker's ultimate goal. It's the code that performs the actual malicious action, such as:

- Gaining unauthorized access to the system.
- Stealing sensitive data.
- Installing a backdoor.
- Launching a denial-of-service attack.
- Executing arbitrary commands.
- Modifying system settings
- Using the computer to mine for cryptocurrency

Let's use an analogy to illustrate this chain:

Imagine a house with a broken window (the *vulnerability*). A burglar uses a screwdriver (the *exploit*) to pry open the window and gain entry. Once inside, they steal valuable possessions (the *payload*).

Common Types of Vulnerabilities: A Closer Look

Let's explore some of the most common types of vulnerabilities that you'll encounter:

- **Buffer Overflows:**

  Occur when a program writes data beyond the boundaries of a buffer, potentially overwriting other parts of memory. This can lead to unpredictable behavior, including crashes, data corruption, or even the execution of arbitrary code.

  Buffer overflows are often caused by programming errors, such as not properly validating the size of input data.

- **SQL Injection (SQLi):**

  Occurs when an attacker injects malicious SQL code into a database query. This can allow the attacker to bypass authentication, steal data, or even modify the database. We touched on this earlier.

- **Cross-Site Scripting (XSS):**

Occurs when an attacker injects malicious JavaScript code into a website, which is then executed by other users who visit the site. The goal is to steal credentials, cookies, or other data.
We touched on this earlier.

- **Remote Code Execution (RCE):**

  Allows an attacker to execute arbitrary code on a remote system. This is one of the most dangerous types of vulnerabilities, as it gives the attacker complete control over the target system.

- **Denial-of-Service (DoS):**

  An attack that aims to make a system or network unavailable to legitimate users. This can be achieved by flooding the target with traffic, consuming its resources, or exploiting a vulnerability that causes it to crash.

- **Authentication Bypass:**

  Occurs when an attacker finds a way to bypass the normal authentication process, allowing them to gain unauthorized access to a system or application.

[Personal Insight Placeholder 1: I've found that understanding the root cause of vulnerabilities is crucial for preventing future attacks. It's not enough to just patch the vulnerability; you also need to fix the underlying problem that allowed it to occur.]

Defensive Thinking: How to Prevent Exploitation

Understanding vulnerabilities and exploits is not just for attackers. As a security professional or ethical hacker, you need to know how to identify and prevent these weaknesses.

Here are some key defensive principles:

- **Secure Coding Practices:** Follow secure coding practices to minimize the risk of introducing vulnerabilities into your code.
- **Input Validation:** Always validate user input to prevent malicious data from being processed by your applications.
- **Regular Security Audits:** Conduct regular security audits to identify potential vulnerabilities in your systems.

- **Patch Management:** Keep your software up-to-date with the latest security patches.
- **Principle of Least Privilege:** Grant users only the minimum privileges required to perform their tasks.
- **Defense in Depth:** Implement multiple layers of security controls to protect your systems.
- **Intrusion Detection Systems (IDS):** Use IDS to monitor for suspicious activity and detect potential attacks.

Putting It Into Perspective: Vulnerability Assessment

A vulnerability assessment can determine the effect of a potential vulnerability. The goal is to find ways to mitigate the risk.

In Summary:

Understanding vulnerabilities and exploits is crucial for any security professional or ethical hacker. By learning how attackers think and what techniques they use, you can better protect your systems from attack. Remember to use this knowledge responsibly and ethically, and always prioritize the security and privacy of others. There are more considerations in an actual deployment versus just running automated tools. What specific areas can we discuss further?

7.2 Brute-Forcing SSH Logins: A Hands-On Example (Ethical Hacking Only!)

Password cracking is a skill needed for ethical hacking. The most straightforward is a brute-force attack, which involves trying all possible combinations of characters until you find the correct password.

However, before we proceed, let's reiterate the *most important* rule:

Disclaimer: Brute-forcing SSH logins without explicit authorization is illegal and unethical. This example is for educational purposes only and should only be used on systems that you own or have explicit permission to test.

We will walk through some test cases and how to implement them.

The Challenge: Cracking Weak Passwords

Brute-forcing is effective because many users still choose weak or easily guessable passwords. This makes it possible for attackers to gain unauthorized access to systems by simply trying a large number of common passwords.

The Tool: Hydra - Your Password-Cracking Companion

Hydra is a powerful password cracking tool that supports a wide range of protocols, including SSH, FTP, HTTP, and more. It's a command-line tool that allows you to specify a target host, a username, and a list of passwords to try.

- **Installing Hydra:**

  If Hydra is not already installed on your Kali Linux system, you can install it using the following command:

  ```
  sudo apt install hydra
  ```

- **Basic Usage:**

  To use Hydra to brute-force an SSH login, you can use the following command:

  ```
  hydra -l <username> -P <password_list> ssh://<target_ip>
  ```

  - <username>: The username to brute-force.
  - <password_list>: The path to a file containing a list of potential passwords (a wordlist).
  - <target_ip>: The IP address of the SSH server.

  Example:

  ```
  hydra -l testuser -P passwords.txt ssh://192.168.1.100
  ```

  This command will attempt to brute-force the SSH login for the testuser account on the host 192.168.1.100 using the passwords in the passwords.txt file.

Understanding the Output:

If Hydra is successful, it will display the correct username and password.

- **More Advanced Techniques:**
    - -t <number>: Specifies the number of concurrent connections to use. Increasing the number of connections can speed up the attack, but it can also make it more detectable.

```
hydra -l testuser -P passwords.txt -t 16 ssh://192.168.1.100
```

This command will use 16 concurrent connections.

    - -vV: Enables verbose output, showing each login attempt.

```
hydra -l testuser -P passwords.txt -vV ssh://192.168.1.100
```

This command will display each login attempt as it is made.

Writing a Bash Script to Automate the Process:

While you can run Hydra directly from the command line, it's often useful to create a Bash script to automate the process. This allows you to easily run the same attack multiple times or to integrate it into a larger workflow.

```
#!/bin/bash

# Set the target host, username, and wordlist
host=$1
username=$2
wordlist=$3

# Check if the required arguments are specified
if [ -z "$host" ] || [ -z "$username" ] || [ -z "$wordlist"
]; then
    echo "Usage: $0 <host> <username> <wordlist>"
    exit 1
fi

# Perform dictionary attack
echo "Performing dictionary attack against
$username@$host..."
hydra -l "$username" -P "$wordlist" ssh://"$host" -t 16 -vV
echo "Password cracking complete."
exit 0
```

This script takes the target host, username, and wordlist as command-line arguments and then runs Hydra with the specified options. It provides a more convenient way to launch the attack.

I've seen firsthand how effective brute-force attacks can be against systems with weak passwords. It's a reminder that even basic security measures can make a big difference.]

Defensive Measures: Protecting Your Systems

Understanding how brute-force attacks work is essential for defending your systems against them. Here are some key defensive measures:

- **Enforce Strong Password Policies:** Require users to choose strong and unique passwords that are difficult to guess.
- **Implement Account Lockout Policies:** Lock out accounts after a certain number of failed login attempts.
- **Use Multi-Factor Authentication (MFA):** Add an extra layer of security to your accounts by requiring users to provide multiple forms of authentication.
- **Monitor for Suspicious Activity:** Monitor your systems for suspicious activity, such as repeated failed login attempts from the same IP address.
- **Use Intrusion Detection Systems (IDS):** Implement an intrusion detection system to detect and respond to brute-force attacks.
- **Limit Access:** Limit SSH access to only those who need it.
- **Use Key-Based Authentication:** Use key-based authentication instead of passwords for SSH access.
- **Change the Default Port:** Change SSH's default port from 22 to another number.

This will help prevent the systems from being hacked.

Understanding the Dangers, Embracing Ethical Hacking

I want to reiterate that brute-forcing SSH logins without explicit permission is illegal and unethical. This knowledge should only be used to test the security of systems that you own or have permission to test.

By understanding how brute-force attacks work and implementing appropriate defensive measures, you can help protect your systems from attack.

7.3 Exploiting a Basic Vulnerable Web Application (SQLi, XSS- Conceptual): A Window into Web Security

Web applications are a frequent target for attackers because a successful intrusion can be costly. By understanding the web applications, you can identify security vulnerabilities that might exist.

As a reminder, please keep ethical in mind. Only run these test on networks/devices that you own or have permission to work with.

Setting Up Your Environment: Damn Vulnerable Web Application (DVWA)

To learn about web application vulnerabilities, you need a safe and controlled environment to experiment. One excellent option is Damn Vulnerable Web Application (DVWA), a deliberately vulnerable web application designed for security training and testing.

1. **Download and Install DVWA:**

   You can download DVWA from the official website or from GitHub.

2. **Configure DVWA:**

   Follow the instructions in the DVWA documentation to configure the database connection and set up the application.
   You will need php and MySql up and running to get this program to work.

It also needs to be run as a super user.

The program includes common web hacking techniques.

SQL Injection: Injecting Malice into the Database

SQL injection (SQLi) occurs when an attacker injects malicious SQL code into a database query, allowing them to bypass authentication, steal data, or even modify the database. It's a classic and still prevalent web application vulnerability.

- **Understanding the Vulnerability:**

SQLi vulnerabilities typically occur when web applications do not properly validate user input before using it in a database query. This allows an attacker to inject arbitrary SQL code into the query, which is then executed by the database server.

Consider a login form that uses the following SQL query to authenticate users:

```
SELECT * FROM users WHERE username = '$username' AND password
= '$password'
```

If the web application does not properly sanitize the username and password variables, an attacker could inject malicious SQL code into these variables to bypass authentication.

- **The Attack:**

  An attacker could enter the following values for username and password:

```
username: ' OR '1'='1
password: ' OR '1'='1
```

  This would result in the following SQL query:

```
SELECT * FROM users WHERE username = '' OR '1'='1' AND
password = '' OR '1'='1'
```

  Because '1'='1' is always true, this query would return all rows from the users table, effectively bypassing authentication. This shows the damage it can cause in a system.

- **Mitigation Techniques:**
    1. **Input Validation:** Sanitize all user input before using it in a database query.
    2. Escape special characters like single quotes ('), double quotes ("), backslashes (\), and null bytes (\0).
    3. Use a whitelist of allowed characters or patterns for each input field.
    4. **Parameterized Queries (Prepared Statements):** Use parameterized queries or prepared statements to separate the SQL code from the

user input. This prevents the user input from being interpreted as SQL code.
5. Use parameterized queries or prepared statements provided by your database library.
6. Use placeholders in the SQL query and bind the user-provided values to these placeholders.
7. **Least Privilege Principle:** Grant database users only the minimum privileges required to perform their tasks.
8. Create separate database users for different parts of your application with specific permissions.
9. Avoid using the root or administrator user for routine operations.
10. **Web Application Firewalls (WAFs):** Implement a WAF to detect and block SQL injection attacks.
11. Use a WAF to filter out malicious requests before they reach your application.
12. Configure your WAF with rules specifically designed to detect and prevent SQL injection attempts.
13. **Regular Security Audits:** Conduct regular security audits to identify potential SQL injection vulnerabilities.
14. Perform code reviews to identify areas where user input is not properly validated or sanitized.
15. Use automated tools to scan your application for SQL injection vulnerabilities.

Important: Never store passwords in plain text. Always hash them using a strong hashing algorithm.

Cross-Site Scripting (XSS): Injecting Malice into the Browser

Cross-site scripting (XSS) occurs when an attacker injects malicious JavaScript code into a website, which is then executed by other users who visit the site. This can allow the attacker to steal cookies, redirect users to malicious websites, or deface the website.

- **Understanding the Vulnerability:**

  XSS vulnerabilities typically occur when web applications do not properly sanitize user input before displaying it on a web page. This allows an attacker to inject arbitrary HTML or JavaScript code into the page, which is then executed by the user's browser.

  Consider the following code snippet:

```
<h1>Welcome, <?php echo $_GET['username']; ?>!</h1>
```

If the web application does not properly sanitize the username parameter, an attacker could inject malicious JavaScript code into this parameter.

- **The Attack:**

  An attacker could enter the following URL:

  ```
  http://example.com/welcome.php?username=<script>alert('XSS')<
  /script>
  ```

  This would result in the following HTML code being displayed on the page:

  ```
  <h1>Welcome, <script>alert('XSS')</script>!</h1>
  ```

  When a user visits this page, the JavaScript code would be executed, displaying an alert box with the message "XSS".

  Types of XSS

1. **Persistent (Stored) XSS**: Where injected scripts are stored on the target server. It occurs when the data provided by the attacker is saved by the server, for example in a database, and then permanently displayed on pages returned to other users in the normal course of browsing, without proper HTML escaping.
    1. A forum can be used. The payload can be stored in a thread and show up every time a user views a thread.
2. **Reflected XSS:** Where the injected script is reflected off the web server, such as in an error message, search result, or any other response that includes as part of the request. This is particularly dangerous.
3. **DOM-based XSS:** Exploits vulnerabilities in client-side code rather than server-side code. In this type of XSS attack, the malicious script is executed because of modifications to the DOM environment in the victim's browser.

- **Mitigation Techniques:**
    1. **Input Sanitization:**
       Sanitize all user input before displaying it on a web page.

2. Use a context-aware output encoding technique to escape special characters like <, >, &, " , and ' based on the output context (HTML, JavaScript, URL, etc.).
3. Remove or encode any potentially harmful HTML tags or attributes, such as <script>, <iframe>, onload, etc.
4. Use a whitelist of allowed HTML tags and attributes if you need to allow some HTML content.
5. **Output Encoding (Escaping):**
   Use a context-aware output encoding technique to escape special characters based on the output context (HTML, JavaScript, URL, etc.).
6. Encode HTML entities for displaying user input in HTML content (e.g., < becomes <, > becomes >).
7. Encode JavaScript strings for displaying user input in JavaScript code (e.g., escape single quotes, double quotes, and backslashes).
8. URL-encode user input for use in URLs.
9. **Content Security Policy (CSP):**
   Use CSP to restrict the sources from which the browser can load resources.
10. Configure your web server to send the Content-Security-Policy HTTP header.
11. Use directives like default-src, script-src, style-src, img-src, etc., to specify the allowed sources for each type of resource.
12. Use 'self' to allow resources from the same origin, and avoid using 'unsafe-inline' and 'unsafe-eval' unless absolutely necessary.
13. **HTTPOnly Cookie Attribute:**
    Set the HTTPOnly attribute for cookies that contain sensitive information (e.g., session IDs).
14. This prevents client-side scripts (JavaScript) from accessing the cookie, reducing the risk of session hijacking.
15. Configure your web server or application framework to set the HTTPOnly attribute for relevant cookies.
16. **Regular Security Audits:**
    Conduct regular security audits to identify potential XSS vulnerabilities.
17. Perform code reviews to identify areas where user input is not properly sanitized or encoded.
18. Use automated tools to scan your application for XSS vulnerabilities.

[I've seen XSS used to deface websites, steal user credentials, and even launch more sophisticated attacks. It's a deceptively simple vulnerability that can have devastating consequences.]

In Summary:

Understanding web application vulnerabilities like SQL injection and XSS is crucial for securing your web applications. By following secure coding practices and implementing appropriate defensive measures, you can significantly reduce the risk

7.4 Introduction to Metasploit (Brief Overview, No Deep Dive): The Hacker's Toolkit on Steroids

You've explored individual vulnerabilities and seen how exploits can be used to take advantage of them. Now, let's introduce a tool that consolidates and automates much of this process: Metasploit. Think of Metasploit as the "kitchen sink" of exploitation frameworks – it's got almost everything you need to plan, execute, and manage exploitation attempts.

What is Metasploit? A Framework for Ethical Hacking

Metasploit is a powerful, open-source framework that provides a wide range of tools and modules for penetration testing, security auditing, and exploit development. Developed by Rapid7, it has become an industry standard and a must-know for anyone serious about cybersecurity (on either the offensive or defensive side).

Disclaimer: It is crucial to remember that Metasploit, like any powerful tool, can be used for both good and evil. Only use Metasploit for ethical purposes, such as penetration testing and security auditing, and only with explicit permission from the system owner.

Key Benefits of Using Metasploit:

- **Centralized Framework:** Provides a single platform for performing various tasks, from reconnaissance to post-exploitation.
- **Modular Design:** Consists of interchangeable modules for different purposes (exploits, payloads, auxiliary modules).
- **Large and Growing Database:** Regularly updated with new exploits and modules, keeping you up-to-date with the latest vulnerabilities.
- **Automation:** Automates many of the steps involved in the exploitation process, making it easier and faster to compromise systems.
- **Reporting:** Provides comprehensive reporting capabilities to document your findings.
- **Easy-to-use Interface:** Metasploit includes a user-friendly console interface, making it easy to navigate and use.

Core Components of Metasploit: The Building Blocks

Metasploit's power comes from its modular design. Here are some of the key module types you'll encounter:

- **Exploits:** Modules that take advantage of known vulnerabilities in software, hardware, or network configurations. They are designed to gain initial access to a target system.
- **Payloads:** The malicious code that is delivered by the exploit and executed on the target system. Payloads can be used to perform a variety of actions, such as gaining remote access, stealing data, or installing a backdoor. There are two main types of payloads:
    - **Staged Payloads:** Transfer a small initial payload (the stager) to the target, which then downloads the rest of the payload (the stage). This is useful for bypassing firewalls and intrusion detection systems.
    - **Single Payloads:** Contain the entire payload in a single module. This is simpler but may be more easily detected.
- **Auxiliary Modules:** Tools for performing reconnaissance, scanning, fuzzing, and other supporting tasks. They are used to gather information about the target system or to prepare for exploitation.
- **Encoders:** Used to encode payloads to evade detection by antivirus software and intrusion detection systems.
- **Listeners:** Used to listen for incoming connections from exploited systems.

Getting Started: The msfconsole

The primary way to interact with Metasploit is through the msfconsole command-line interface.

1. **Launch the msfconsole:**

   Open a terminal on your Kali Linux system and type msfconsole.

   ```
   msfconsole
   ```

   This will launch the Metasploit console, which provides a prompt for entering commands.

2. **Searching for Modules:**

You can search for modules using the search command. For example, to search for modules related to SSH, you can type:

```
search ssh
```

This will display a list of all modules that are related to SSH, including exploits, auxiliary modules, and payloads.

3. **Using Modules:**

   To use a module, you first need to select it using the use command. For example, to use the auxiliary/scanner/ssh/ssh_version module, you can type:

   ```
   use auxiliary/scanner/ssh/ssh_version
   ```

   This will select the ssh_version module and display its options.

4. **Setting Options:**

   Each module has a set of options that you need to configure before running the module. You can view the options using the show options command.

   ```
   show options
   ```

   This will display a list of the module's options, along with their current values and descriptions.

   You can set the value of an option using the set command. For example, to set the RHOSTS option to 192.168.1.100, you can type:

   ```
   set RHOSTS 192.168.1.100
   ```

5. **Running the Module:**

   Once you have configured all of the required options, you can run the module using the run or exploit command.

   ```
   run
   ```

This will execute the module and display the results.

A Simple Example: Scanning for SSH Versions:

Let's use Metasploit to scan a target host for its SSH version:

1. **Launch msfconsole:**

   ```
   msfconsole
   ```

2. **Search for the SSH version scanner module:**

   ```
   search ssh_version
   ```

3. **Select the auxiliary/scanner/ssh/ssh_version module:**

   ```
   use auxiliary/scanner/ssh/ssh_version
   ```

4. **Show the module options:**

   ```
   show options
   ```

5. **Set the RHOSTS option to the target IP address:**

   ```
   set RHOSTS 192.168.1.100
   ```

6. **Run the module:**

   ```
   run
   ```

The output will display the SSH version running on the target host (if it's running an SSH server).

A Word of Caution:

Metasploit is a powerful tool that should be used responsibly and ethically. Always obtain explicit permission before using Metasploit on a target system.

[I've found that Metasploit is an invaluable tool for penetration testing, but it's important to remember that it's just one tool in your arsenal. You still need to understand the underlying concepts and techniques to be an effective security professional.]

Beyond the Basics: Meterpreter

One of Metasploit's most powerful features is Meterpreter, an advanced payload that provides a wide range of post-exploitation capabilities. Meterpreter allows you to:

- Browse the file system
- Download and upload files
- Execute commands
- Capture keystrokes
- Take screenshots
- Migrate to other processes
- Pivot to other networks

To use Meterpreter, you need to select a Meterpreter payload when configuring your exploit module. Once the exploit is successful, you will gain a Meterpreter session, which provides a command-line interface for interacting with the compromised system.

In Summary:

Metasploit is a powerful and versatile framework that can significantly simplify the process of penetration testing and security auditing. By understanding its core components and learning how to use its modules effectively, you can greatly enhance your ability to assess and improve the security of your systems. However, remember to use Metasploit responsibly and ethically, always obtaining explicit permission before testing a target system. You are ready for the next chapter!

Chapter 8: System Hardening & Security Best Practices: Building a Fortress

You've learned how to think like an attacker, identify vulnerabilities, and even exploit them (ethically, of course!). Now, it's time to switch gears and focus on defense. This chapter is all about system hardening, which involves implementing security measures to reduce the attack surface and make it more difficult for attackers to compromise your systems. Think of it as building a fortress to protect your valuable assets. This is one of the most important tasks in creating a secure system.

8.1 Secure Password Management: The First Line of Defense-Defending the Gate

Passwords are the most common method to protect your computer. They provide the first step in gaining unauthorized access. Weak passwords are the bane of security professionals. Strong passwords are the first line of defense against unauthorized access.

What makes passwords strong?

Strong Password Policies: Setting the Bar High

Enforce strong password policies to ensure that users choose passwords that are difficult to guess. This includes:

- **Minimum Length:**
  - Require passwords to be at least 12 characters long. Longer is better, and 16+ is ideal.
  - The longer the password, the more difficult it is to crack using brute-force attacks.
- **Complexity:**
  - Require passwords to include a combination of uppercase and lowercase letters, numbers, and symbols.
  - This increases the number of possible password combinations, making it more difficult to crack.
- **Uniqueness:**
  - Prohibit users from reusing passwords or using passwords that are similar to previous passwords.

- Password reuse is a major security risk, as attackers can use credentials from one compromised account to access other accounts.
- **Regular Changes:**
  - Require users to change their passwords regularly (e.g., every 90 days).
  - This reduces the window of opportunity for attackers to use compromised credentials.
- **Prohibition of Obvious Passwords:**
  - This includes names and pet names.

Implementation: The Technical Details

On Linux systems, you can enforce password complexity requirements using the pam_cracklib module. This module checks passwords against a variety of criteria, such as length, complexity, and dictionary words.

1. **Edit the /etc/pam.d/common-password file:**

   Open the /etc/pam.d/common-password file in a text editor with root privileges:

   ```
   sudo nano /etc/pam.d/common-password
   ```

2. **Add the pam_cracklib module:**

   Add the following line to the /etc/pam.d/common-password file:

   ```
   password         requisite
   pam_cracklib.so retry=3 minlen=12 ucredit=-1 lcredit=-1
   dcredit=-1 ocredit=-1
   ```

   This line configures pam_cracklib to:

   - retry=3: Allow the user to retry entering a password 3 times.
   - minlen=12: Require a minimum password length of 12 characters.
   - ucredit=-1: Require at least one uppercase character.
   - lcredit=-1: Require at least one lowercase character.
   - dcredit=-1: Require at least one digit.
   - ocredit=-1: Require at least one other character (symbol).
3. **Save the file and exit the text editor.**

In nano, press Ctrl+X, then Y, then Enter to save and exit.
This forces the system to generate strong passwords that are harder to break.

Salt and Hash, Salt and Hash: Securing Stored Passwords

Storing passwords in plain text is a recipe for disaster. If an attacker gains access to your password database, they will have access to all of your users' passwords. Always hash passwords using a strong hashing algorithm, such as bcrypt or Argon2. Salting adds a unique random value to each password before hashing, making it more difficult for attackers to use precomputed tables of password hashes (rainbow tables).

- **Bcrypt:** A widely used password hashing algorithm that is designed to be slow and computationally expensive, making it more difficult to crack passwords.
- **Argon2:** A newer password hashing algorithm that is designed to be even more resistant to attacks than bcrypt.

Most modern programming languages and frameworks provide built-in support for password hashing. Always use the recommended password hashing library for your language or framework.

```
import bcrypt

password = b"mysecretpassword"
hashed_password = bcrypt.hashpw(password, bcrypt.gensalt())
print(hashed_password)
```

[Personal Insight Placeholder 1: I've seen too many breaches caused by plain text or poorly hashed passwords. It's a basic security principle that is often overlooked, but it's absolutely essential for protecting your users' data.]

Password Managers: Empowering Users to Create and Manage Strong Passwords

Password managers are software applications that allow users to securely store and manage their passwords. They can generate strong, unique passwords for each website or application and then store them in an encrypted vault.

Encourage users to use password managers. This makes it easier for them to follow strong password policies without having to memorize a large number of complex passwords.

- **Benefits of Using Password Managers:**
    - **Strong Passwords:** Password managers can generate strong, unique passwords for each website or application.
    - **Secure Storage:** Password managers store passwords in an encrypted vault, protecting them from unauthorized access.
    - **Convenience:** Password managers automatically fill in passwords when you visit a website or application, making it easier and faster to log in.
- **Popular Password Managers:**
    - LastPass
    - 1Password
    - Bitwarden
    - KeePass (open-source)

Multi-Factor Authentication (MFA): Adding an Extra Layer of Security

Multi-factor authentication (MFA) adds an extra layer of security to your accounts by requiring users to provide multiple forms of authentication. This can include something they know (e.g., a password), something they have (e.g., a security token or smartphone), or something they are (e.g., a fingerprint).

Implementing MFA can significantly reduce the risk of unauthorized access, even if an attacker manages to crack a user's password.

- **Common MFA Methods:**
    - **SMS Codes:** Sending a verification code to the user's phone via SMS.
    - **Authenticator Apps:** Using an authenticator app (e.g., Google Authenticator, Authy) to generate time-based one-time passwords (TOTP).
    - **Hardware Security Keys:** Using a physical security key (e.g., YubiKey) to verify the user's identity.
    - **Biometrics:** Using a fingerprint or facial recognition to verify the user's identity.

These methods are generally very robust!

Key Takeaways:

- **Enforce Strong Password Policies:** Set the bar high for password complexity and uniqueness.

- **Salt and Hash Passwords:** Always hash passwords using a strong hashing algorithm and a unique salt.
- **Encourage Password Managers:** Promote the use of password managers to help users create and manage strong passwords.
- **Implement Multi-Factor Authentication:** Add an extra layer of security with MFA.
- **Educate Users:** Educate users about the importance of secure password management practices.

How can we further improve the password strength of a machine?

8.2 User Account Security: Limiting Privileges- The Principle of Least Privilege

Now that we've locked down passwords, let's focus on another critical aspect of system hardening: limiting user privileges.

The Principle of Least Privilege (PoLP): The Cornerstone of Security

The Principle of Least Privilege (PoLP) is a security principle that states that users should only be granted the minimum privileges required to perform their tasks. This reduces the attack surface and limits the damage that an attacker can cause if they compromise an account. To fully understand this: give employees the tools and network permissions to do their job and *nothing more.*

Think of it as giving someone a key only to the rooms they need to access in a building, rather than giving them the master key to the entire building.

Why is Limiting Privileges Important?

- **Reduced Attack Surface:** The more privileges an account has, the more potential attack vectors an attacker can exploit.
- **Limited Damage:** If an attacker compromises an account with limited privileges, they will only be able to access a limited set of resources.
- **Improved Accountability:** By assigning specific privileges to each user, you can better track who is accessing what resources and identify any suspicious activity.

Practical Steps for Implementing Least Privilege:

1. **Disable Unnecessary Accounts: Clean House**

Disable or remove any unnecessary user accounts on your systems, such as guest accounts, default accounts, or accounts that are no longer in use.

On Linux systems, you can use the userdel command to remove a user account:

```
sudo userdel <username>
```

Replace <username> with the name of the user account you want to remove.

You can also disable an account by locking it, which prevents the user from logging in.

```
sudo passwd -l <username>
```

This command will lock the specified user account.

It may be possible to setup automatic archival by scripting a job.

2. **Limit Administrator Privileges: Keep Root Access Secure**

   Limit the number of users who have administrator (root) privileges. Only grant administrator privileges to those who absolutely need them.

   On Linux systems, administrator privileges are typically granted through membership in the sudo group. You can use the gpasswd command to add or remove users from the sudo group:

```
sudo gpasswd -a <username> sudo   # Add user to sudo group
sudo gpasswd -d <username> sudo   # Remove user from sudo
group
```

   Replace <username> with the name of the user account you want to add or remove from the sudo group.

   You can also customize which commands users can run with sudo by editing the /etc/sudoers file. However, be very careful when editing this file, as incorrect syntax can lock you out of your system. It may also be better to leave it as is unless there are pressing needs.

3. **Use Separate Accounts for Administrative Tasks: Avoid Daily Root Use**

   Create separate accounts for administrative tasks and use them only when necessary. This prevents attackers from gaining access to administrator privileges by compromising a user account that is used for everyday tasks.

   For example, create a dedicated admin account that is only used for performing administrative tasks. Use your regular user account for browsing the web, checking email, and other non-administrative tasks.

   For security, it is helpful to know what commands were run.

4. **Regularly Review User Accounts and Privileges: The Security Audit**

   Regularly review your user accounts and privileges to ensure that they are still appropriate. Remove or disable any accounts that are no longer needed and adjust privileges as necessary.

   This process should be part of your regular security audit.

   - **Listing user accounts:**

     ```
     getent passwd
     ```

   - **Listing the user account with admin access:**

     ```
     getent group sudo
     ```

There is no simple and concise list for checking admin access. It can be more tricky when systems have additional levels of privilege, since the root access is only for some system configurations.

1. **Implement Role-Based Access Control (RBAC): Align Access with Roles**

   ```
   RBAC is a security mechanism that allows you to grant
   permissions based on a user's role within the organization.
   This makes it easier to manage user privileges and ensure
   that users only have access to the resources they need.

   For example, you could create roles for:
   ```

```
*    System Administrators: Full access to all systems and
resources.
*    Security Engineers: Access to security tools and logs.
*    Developers: Access to code repositories and development
environments.
*    Users: Limited access to specific applications and data.
```

Each group will receive access to the tools and logs they need.

I've found that implementing RBAC makes it much easier to manage user privileges and ensure that users only have access to the resources they need. It also makes it easier to audit user activity and identify potential security breaches.]

Practical Implementation: Automating User Management Tasks

You can use Bash scripts to automate many of the user management tasks described above. For example, you could create a script that:

- Creates a new user account with a strong password.
- Adds the user account to the appropriate groups based on their role.
- Configures the user's home directory with the necessary files and permissions.
- Sends the user an email with their login credentials and instructions on how to change their password.

By automating these tasks, you can ensure that all new user accounts are created with consistent security settings.

Key actions to review:

- Disable or remove default accounts
- Create an admin account, if one doesn't exist.
- Lock the root login to prevent users from logging directly into it.
- Use SU to assume super user for admin purposes

In Summary:

Limiting user privileges is a fundamental security best practice that can significantly reduce the attack surface and limit the damage that attackers can cause. By implementing the principles of least privilege and regularly reviewing user accounts and privileges, you can create a more secure and resilient system. You are now another step further. What would you like to investigate next?

8.3 Firewall Configuration (ufw / iptables Basics): Guarding the Gates- Your Network Traffic Cop

A firewall is a security system that monitors and controls incoming and outgoing network traffic based on pre-defined security rules. Think of it as a gatekeeper, only allowing authorized traffic to pass through and blocking everything else. A proper firewall is a must for any secured network, and especially important in ethical hacking.

Why Firewalls Matter: Creating a Network Perimeter

Firewalls are essential for:

- **Preventing Unauthorized Access:** Blocking attackers from accessing your systems.
- **Protecting Against Malware:** Preventing malware from spreading across your network.
- **Controlling Network Traffic:** Limiting network traffic to only what is necessary.
- **Enforcing Security Policies:** Enforcing your organization's security policies.
- **Monitoring Logs:** Providing log data for analysis.

Understanding Firewall Concepts: Rules, Chains, and Tables

Before we dive into specific tools, let's clarify some key firewall concepts:

- **Rules:** Individual statements that define how traffic should be handled (e.g., allowed, blocked, logged).
- **Chains:** A collection of rules that are processed in order. Common chains include INPUT (incoming traffic), OUTPUT (outgoing traffic), and FORWARD (traffic passing through the system).
- **Tables:** A way to organize chains. The most common table is the filter table, which is used for basic filtering of network traffic.

ufw (Uncomplicated Firewall): The User-Friendly Approach

ufw is a user-friendly front-end for iptables that simplifies the process of configuring the firewall. It provides a simple and intuitive interface for managing firewall rules, making it a great choice for beginners.

- **Installation:**

  If ufw is not already installed on your Kali Linux system, you can install it using the following command:

  ```
  sudo apt install ufw
  ```

- **Basic Commands:**
  - **Enabling ufw:**

    ```
    sudo ufw enable
    ```

  - **Disabling ufw:**

    ```
    sudo ufw disable
    ```

- *Warning: Disabling the firewall can expose your system to security risks. Only disable the firewall temporarily for troubleshooting purposes.*
  - **Allowing Traffic:**

```
sudo ufw allow 22/tcp  # Allow SSH traffic
sudo ufw allow 80/tcp  # Allow HTTP traffic
sudo ufw allow 443/tcp # Allow HTTPS traffic
sudo ufw allow from 192.168.1.100 to any port 22 # Allow SSH
from specific IP
```

    Replace 22, 80, and 443 with the port numbers you want to allow. You can also specify the protocol (TCP or UDP).

  - **Denying Traffic:**

```
sudo ufw deny 25/tcp  # Deny SMTP traffic
sudo ufw deny from 192.168.1.0/24 to any port 22 #Deny SSH
from an entire subnet
```

    Replace 25 with the port number you want to deny.

  - **Checking Status:**

```
sudo ufw status
```

This command displays the current firewall rules.

- **Deleting Rules:**

  To delete a rule from the firewall, first, you will have to list all rules and their numbering using the command sudo ufw status numbered.

  After identifying the number, you wish to delete, you may use the command sudo ufw delete [number].

You may need to run these commands from the super user.

Important: When enabling ufw, make sure to allow SSH traffic first. Otherwise, you may lock yourself out of your system.

[Personal Insight Placeholder 1: I've found that a well-configured firewall is one of the most effective ways to protect your systems from attack. It's essential to understand the principles of firewall configuration and to regularly review your firewall rules to ensure that they are still appropriate.]

iptables (Advanced Firewall): Fine-Grained Control

iptables is a powerful but more complex firewall that is built into the Linux kernel. It provides a flexible and granular way to manage firewall rules, but it can be more challenging to learn and use than ufw. Due to this complexity and specific system needs, it may be a good topic for an advanced book instead of a basic guide.

While this complexity is important, in certain high-security environments, security administrators manually write scripts to run complex systems.

```
iptables -A INPUT -p tcp --dport 22 -j ACCEPT
```

Best Practices for Firewall Configuration:

- **Default Deny Policy:** Start with a default deny policy, which blocks all traffic except what is explicitly allowed.
- **Principle of Least Privilege:** Only allow traffic that is necessary for your systems to function.

- **Regularly Review Rules:** Regularly review your firewall rules to ensure that they are still appropriate.
- **Log Everything:** Enable logging to track all network traffic and identify potential security incidents.
- **Test Your Configuration:** Test your firewall configuration to ensure that it is working as expected.
  Use these functions in a separate script to load automatically on machine start.

In Summary:

Firewalls are a critical component of any security infrastructure. By understanding the principles of firewall configuration and using tools like ufw and iptables, you can effectively control network traffic and protect your systems from unauthorized access. You can implement the learnings in the prior chapters to improve your system. In what ways would you like to improve the system?

8.4 Keeping Your System Updated: Patching Vulnerabilities- Staying Ahead of the Curve

Software is complex. There's always the possibility of vulnerabilities cropping up that can expose your systems to risk.

Why Software Updates are Critical: Plugging the Holes

Keeping your software up-to-date is one of the most important things you can do to maintain the security of your systems. Software updates often include security patches that fix known vulnerabilities. Installing these updates promptly can prevent attackers from exploiting these vulnerabilities and compromising your systems.

The longer you take to patch a vulnerability, the more time attackers have to exploit it.

Key Strategies for Staying Updated:

1. **Understanding the Update Process: Package Managers to the Rescue**

   Most modern operating systems use package managers to manage software installations and updates. Package managers provide a centralized way to install, update, and remove software, ensuring that all dependencies are met and that the system remains consistent.

On Debian-based systems (like Kali Linux), the apt package manager is used.

2. **Automated Updates: Set It and (Mostly) Forget It**

   Configure your system to automatically install security updates. This is the easiest way to ensure that your systems are always up-to-date with the latest security patches.

   On Debian-based systems, you can use the unattended-upgrades package to automate security updates.

   - **Install unattended-upgrades:**

     ```
     sudo apt install unattended-upgrades
     ```

   - **Configure unattended-upgrades:**

     ```
     sudo dpkg-reconfigure unattended-upgrades
     ```

     This will prompt you to configure unattended-upgrades. Select "Yes" to enable automatic security updates.

     You can also edit the /etc/apt/apt.conf.d/50unattended-upgrades file to customize the update process.

   The automatic update process will be used when available.

3. **Manual Checks and Updates: Taking Control**

   Even if you have automated updates enabled, it's still a good idea to regularly check for updates manually. This allows you to:

   - **Verify Updates:** Confirm that updates are being installed correctly.
   - **Install Non-Security Updates:** Install updates that are not classified as security updates, but may still include important bug fixes or new features.
   - **Address Urgent Vulnerabilities:** Install updates that address critical vulnerabilities that require immediate attention.

To check for and install updates manually, use the following commands:

```
sudo apt update
sudo apt upgrade
```

contsudo apt update: Updates the package lists from the software repositories.

- sudo apt upgrade: Upgrades all installed packages to the latest versions.

4. **Staying Informed: Security Mailing Lists and Newsletters**

   Subscribe to security mailing lists and newsletters to stay informed about the latest vulnerabilities and security updates. This will help you to identify systems that require immediate attention.

   Some useful resources include:

   - **The Kali Linux Security Mailing List:** https://www.kali.org/community/
   - **The National Vulnerability Database (NVD):** https://nvd.nist.gov/

5. **Document All Steps Taken:**

   Make sure you include steps for what to do during regular patch management and testing. Make sure you have systems to roll back the changes in case something breaks.

[I make it a habit to check for updates on my systems at least once a week. It's a small investment of time that can pay off big in terms of security.]

Practical Implications: A Real-World Example

Imagine a critical vulnerability is discovered in a popular web server software. If you have automated updates enabled, your system will automatically download and install the security patch, protecting your web server from attack. If you don't have automated updates enabled, you'll need to manually check for updates and install the patch. The delay in patching the vulnerability could give attackers time to exploit it and compromise your web server.

Special Considerations:

- **Testing Updates:** Before deploying updates to production systems, it's a good idea to test them in a staging environment to ensure that they don't introduce any new problems. This is also called a "Blue-Green" deployment.
- **Rebooting Systems:** Some updates require a system reboot to take effect. Be sure to schedule reboots during off-peak hours to minimize disruption to users.
- **Third-Party Software:** Don't forget to update third-party software, such as web browsers, PDF readers, and other applications. These applications can also contain vulnerabilities that can be exploited by attackers.

Automating Manual Steps - the best of both worlds

Here is how to automate this:

```
#!/bin/bash
echo "Begin system update:"
sudo apt update
If [ $? -eq 0 ]; then
 sudo apt upgrade -y
 echo "System updated"
Elif [ $? != 0 ]; then
 Echo "System has errors, please review"
 Fi

Echo "Finished system update"
```

That would have to be customized per system, but it gets the idea across.

In Summary:

Keeping your systems updated with the latest security patches is essential for protecting against vulnerabilities and maintaining a secure environment. By automating updates, staying informed, and following best practices, you can minimize the risk of attack and ensure that your systems are always up-to-date. After automating system checks and balances, it's time for other security tips. What are other security considerations for users?

8.5 Disabling Unnecessary Services: Shrinking the Target - Minimizing Your Exposure

Every service running on your system is a potential attack vector. Even if a service is properly configured and patched, it can still be exploited if an attacker discovers a new vulnerability. That's why disabling unnecessary services is a crucial step in system hardening. Think of it as removing unnecessary doors and windows from a building, making it more difficult for attackers to gain entry.

Why Reduce the Attack Surface? Less is More (Secure)

The attack surface is the sum of all the potential entry points that an attacker can use to compromise a system. By reducing the attack surface, you are:

- **Minimizing Exposure:** Fewer services running means fewer potential vulnerabilities.
- **Reducing Complexity:** A simpler system is easier to manage and secure.
- **Improving Performance:** Disabling unnecessary services can free up system resources and improve performance.

Identifying Unnecessary Services: Knowing What to Cut

The first step in disabling unnecessary services is to identify which services are actually needed. This requires understanding the purpose of each service and whether it is essential for the system's functionality.

- **List All Active Services:**

  Use the systemctl command to list all active services on your system:

  ```
  systemctl list-units --type=service --state=running
  ```

  This command displays a list of all active services, along with their status and description. The amount of output here can be overwhelming!
  Check to determine which systems have the least number of running processes.

- **Research Each Service:**

For each service, research its purpose and whether it is required for your system's intended use. You can use the systemctl show command to display detailed information about a service:

```
systemctl show <service_name>
```

Replace <service_name> with the name of the service you want to investigate.

This command will display a wealth of information about the service, including its description, dependencies, and configuration.

You can also use online resources, such as the ArchWiki, to find information about specific services.

- **Example Services to Consider Disabling:**
    - **Bluetooth:** If you don't use Bluetooth, you can disable the bluetooth.service.
    - **Printing Services (CUPS):** If you don't need to print, you can disable the cups.service.
    - **Mail Transfer Agent (Sendmail/Postfix):** If you don't need to send email from your system, you can disable the sendmail or postfix services.
    - **Web Server (Apache/Nginx):** If you're not hosting a website, you can disable the apache2 or nginx services.

Important: Be careful when disabling services. Disabling essential services can cause your system to malfunction. Always research a service before disabling it to ensure that it is not required for your system's core functionality.

Disabling Services: Taking Action

Once you've identified the services you want to disable, you can use the systemctl command to disable them.

- **Stopping a Service:**

  Before disabling a service, it's a good idea to stop it first. This will ensure that the service is not running when you disable it.

```
sudo systemctl stop <service_name>
```

Replace <service_name> with the name of the service you want to stop.

- **Disabling a Service:**

  To disable a service, use the systemctl disable command:

  ```
  sudo systemctl disable <service_name>
  ```

  This command will prevent the service from starting automatically at boot.
  Reversing a Service

  ```
        To reverse a service and allow it to run again, you'll
  have to call the `enable` version.
  ```

  ```
  sudo systemctl enable <service_name>
  ```

In some cases, services may have dependencies on other services. Disabling a service may also disable its dependencies.

Important: It's a good idea to test your system after disabling services to ensure that everything is still working as expected. You can test by running the machine and running any expected functionality.*

[Personal Insight Placeholder 1: I've seen many systems compromised because of unnecessary services running on open ports. It's essential to minimize the attack surface by disabling any services that are not absolutely required.]

Beyond Disabling: Masking Services (Advanced)

In some cases, simply disabling a service may not be enough. Some services may be automatically started by other services or by systemd timers. To prevent these services from starting, you can mask them.

Masking a service prevents it from being started, even if it is a dependency of another service or is started by a systemd timer.

- **Masking a Service:**

```
sudo systemctl mask <service_name>
```

Replace <service_name> with the name of the service you want to mask.

- **Unmasking a Service:**

```
sudo systemctl unmask <service_name>
```

This command will unmask the service, allowing it to be started again.

Use masking with extreme caution, as it can prevent essential services from running.

In Summary:

Disabling unnecessary services is a critical step in system hardening. By carefully identifying and disabling services that are not required for your system's functionality, you can significantly reduce the attack surface and improve the security of your systems. This is a key task that is quick to do and has high security implications.
What is next?

8.6 Introduction to Intrusion Detection: Setting Up the Alarm System

You've fortified your systems with strong passwords, limited privileges, and a well-configured firewall. But even the best defenses can be bypassed. That's why it's essential to have an intrusion detection system (IDS) in place to monitor your systems for suspicious activity and alert you to potential attacks. Think of an IDS as your alarm system, alerting you when someone is trying to break into your fortress.

What is Intrusion Detection? Knowing When You're Under Attack

An intrusion detection system (IDS) is a security tool that monitors network traffic and system activity for malicious or suspicious behavior. It can detect a wide range of attacks, including:

- **Port Scans:** Attempts to identify open ports and services on your systems.
- **Brute-Force Attacks:** Attempts to crack passwords by trying a large number of combinations.

- **Denial-of-Service (DoS) Attacks:** Attempts to make your systems unavailable to legitimate users.
- **Malware Infections:** Attempts to install or execute malicious code on your systems.
- **Unauthorized Access:** Attempts to access sensitive data or resources without authorization.

How Does an IDS Work? Signatures, Anomalies, and More

IDS use a variety of techniques to detect malicious activity:

- **Signature-Based Detection:**

  Compares network traffic and system activity to a database of known attack signatures or patterns. This is like looking for known fingerprints at a crime scene. If the IDS finds a match, it generates an alert.

- **Anomaly-Based Detection:**

  Establishes a baseline of normal network behavior and system activity. Any traffic or activity that deviates significantly from this baseline is flagged as suspicious. This is like detecting a sudden change in someone's behavior that suggests they are up to no good.

- **Policy-Based Detection:**

  Detects violations of predefined security policies. For example, a policy might state that users should not access certain websites or that certain files should not be modified. If the IDS detects a violation of a policy, it generates an alert.

- **Honeypots:**

A trap set to detect, deflect, or, in some manner, counteract attempts at unauthorized use of information systems. Generally, they consist of a computer, data or a network site that appears to be part of the production network, but is actually isolated and monitored, and which seems to contain information or a resource of value to attackers. The tool is used to gather intelligence.

There are two main types of IDS:

- **Host-Based IDS (HIDS):**

  HIDS are installed on individual systems and monitor those systems for suspicious activity. They typically monitor system logs, file integrity, and process activity. One popular HIDS is OSSEC.

- **Network-Based IDS (NIDS):**

  NIDS monitor network traffic for suspicious activity. They typically analyze packet headers, payload data, and network protocols. One popular NIDS is Snort.

[I've found that a combination of HIDS and NIDS provides the best protection against a wide range of attacks. HIDS can detect attacks that originate from within the system, while NIDS can detect attacks that are launched from outside the system.]

Implementing a Basic NIDS with Snort: A Hands-On Example

Snort is a free and open-source NIDS that is widely used by security professionals and network administrators. It's a powerful and flexible tool that can be customized to detect a wide range of attacks.

Disclaimer: Before running a tool, please familiarize yourself with security regulations. Snort will consume significant processing power.

1. **Install Snort:**

   If Snort is not already installed on your Kali Linux system, you can install it using the following command:

   ```
   sudo apt install snort
   ```

2. **Configure Snort:**

   The Snort configuration file is located at /etc/snort/snort.conf. You can edit this file to customize Snort's behavior, such as specifying the network interfaces to monitor, the rules to use, and the actions to take when an alert is generated.

   Some important configuration options include:

- var RULE_PATH: Specifies the directory where Snort rules are located.
- var HOME_NET: Specifies the IP address range of your home network.
- var EXTERNAL_NET: Specifies the IP address range of the external network (usually any).

3. **Download Snort Rules:**

   Snort uses rules to detect malicious activity. You can download a variety of Snort rule sets from the Snort website or from other sources.

   To download the Snort community rules, you can use the oinkmaster tool:

   ```
   sudo apt install oinkmaster
   sudo oinkmaster -o /etc/snort/rules -u <your_oink_code>
   ```

   Replace <your_oink_code> with your Snort Oink code. You can obtain a Snort Oink code by registering on the Snort website. If you did not purchase, then leave it blank.

4. **Start Snort:**

   To start Snort, use the following command:

   ```
   sudo snort -dev -i <interface> -c /etc/snort/snort.conf
   ```

   Replace <interface> with the name of the network interface you want to monitor (e.g., eth0, wlan0).

   This command will start Snort in data acquisition (DAQ) mode, which captures network traffic and analyzes it against the Snort rules.

5. Run the service as a deamon.
   The next step is to setup to run in the background without direct interaction.
6. Start the Snort program at start-up
   Finally, you can run enable the Snort program to run at each boot of the system.
7. **Analyze Snort Alerts:**

```
Snort generates alerts when it detects suspicious activity.
The alerts are typically logged to the `/var/log/snort`
directory.

You can use a variety of tools to analyze Snort alerts, such
as:

*    **`snort-stat`:** A command-line tool for summarizing
Snort alerts.
*    **`Snorby`:** A web-based interface for analyzing Snort
alerts.
```

Practical Considerations:

- **Performance Impact:** Running an IDS can have a significant impact on system performance. Carefully consider the resources required to run the IDS and adjust the configuration accordingly. This can also create network bottle necks.
- **False Positives:** IDSs can generate false positives, which are alerts that are not actually malicious. Be prepared to investigate false positives and adjust your IDS rules to minimize their occurrence.
- **Rule Management:** Keeping your IDS rules up-to-date is essential for detecting the latest threats. Regularly update your Snort rules to ensure that you are protected against new attacks.

This is a great first step to learning how to use IDSs for network maintenance and defense.

[I've found that IDSs are an essential tool for detecting and responding to security incidents. However, it's important to remember that they are not a silver bullet. You still need to implement other security measures to protect your systems.]

In Summary:

Intrusion detection systems are essential for monitoring your systems for malicious activity and alerting you to potential attacks. By understanding the different types of IDS and learning how to configure and use them effectively, you can significantly improve the security of your environment. By combining the tools and techniques, you will improve the safety and security of the overall network and the devices connected to it. Which tool should we be exploring next?

Chapter 9: Okay, here's Chapter 9, "Web Application Security Basics," crafted to be informative and practical while emphasizing a conceptual understanding.

Chapter 9: Web Application Security Basics: Defending the Digital Facade

Web applications are the storefronts of the digital world, providing access to services, data, and functionality. However, they are also a prime target for attackers. Understanding web application vulnerabilities and how to prevent them is essential for any security professional or ethical hacker.

Disclaimer: Always test for web vulnerabilities in a controlled environment with explicit authorization. Unauthorized testing can have legal consequences.

9.1 Common Web Vulnerabilities: SQL Injection, XSS, CSRF (Conceptual): Peering into the Web Security Abyss

Web applications form the front line for companies to do business and interact with clients. With a lot at stake, there has to be security.

SQL Injection (SQLi): Bypassing the Gatekeeper

SQL Injection (SQLi) occurs when an attacker can insert malicious SQL code into a database query. A query that should fetch a specific user or data gets manipulated by the addition of code, allowing an attacker unauthorized access. It is a severe vulnerability if not addressed during development.

This often occurs because an application is built from a framework that is new, untested, or not fully understood by the developers.

- **The Underlying Weakness: Untrusted Input**

SQLi exploits trust. It preys on web applications that blindly trust user input, especially from web forms. In these applications, data is directly incorporated into SQL queries without proper sanitization or validation.

```
SELECT * FROM users WHERE username = '$username' AND password =
'$password';
```

The vulnerability lies in the assumption that $username and $password contain legitimate data. Without sanitization, an attacker can manipulate these variables.

- **The Attack in Detail:**

An attacker can craft input that alters the SQL query's logic. For example, injecting ' OR '1'='1 into the username field effectively changes the query to:

```
SELECT * FROM users WHERE username = '' OR '1'='1' AND password =
'$password';
```

The condition '1'='1' is always true. The altered query bypasses the password check, granting the attacker access to the database's first entry by sidestepping user verification. An attacker can then see the list of users and use those credentials to login to the system.

What Damage Can SQLi Do?

The impact can be immense:

1. **Data Breach:** Attackers can exfiltrate entire databases containing sensitive customer data, financial records, and proprietary information.
2. **Data Manipulation:** They can modify existing data, leading to corruption, fraud, or reputational damage.
3. **Privilege Escalation:** Attackers can gain administrative access to the database, allowing them to create new accounts, modify permissions, or even execute arbitrary code on the database server.
4. **Denial of Service (DoS):** Attackers can craft SQL queries that consume excessive resources, rendering the application unusable.

There also instances where database details themselves can be pulled with SQLi from the web applications.

Cross-Site Scripting (XSS): Hijacking the User Experience

Cross-Site Scripting (XSS) allows attackers to inject malicious scripts (typically JavaScript) into web pages viewed by other users. Unlike SQLi, XSS doesn't target the server directly; instead, it exploits the trust between users and a website. This can involve injecting code into forms or pages.

- **The Underlying Weakness: Unsanitized Output**

XSS vulnerabilities arise when web applications display user-provided data without proper encoding or sanitization. This allows attackers to inject arbitrary HTML or

JavaScript code into the page, which is then executed by the user's browser. The most valuable pieces are the credentials, since they can provide elevated access to more systems.

- **The Attack in Detail:**

An attacker injects <script>alert("XSS Attack!");</script> into a website's comment section or a user profile field. When a user visits the affected page, their browser executes the injected script, displaying an alert box.

What Damage Can XSS Do?

The impact can range from nuisance to severe:

1. **Cookie Theft:** Attackers can steal session cookies, allowing them to impersonate users and gain access to their accounts.
2. **Website Redirection:** Attackers can redirect users to malicious websites that phish for credentials or distribute malware.
3. **Website Defacement:** Attackers can modify the content of the website, displaying misleading information or defacing the site with offensive content.
4. **Keylogging:** Attackers can capture user keystrokes, stealing sensitive information such as passwords or credit card numbers.

Cross-Site Request Forgery (CSRF): The Silent Exploiter

CSRF (Cross-Site Request Forgery) is a type of attack where an attacker tricks a user into performing actions on a web application without their knowledge or consent. It exploits the trust that a website has in a user's browser.

- **The Underlying Weakness: Lack of Request Verification**

CSRF vulnerabilities arise when web applications do not properly verify that requests are originating from legitimate users. This allows attackers to craft malicious requests that appear to be legitimate and trick users into executing them.

- **The Attack in Detail:**

An attacker tricks a user into clicking a malicious link or visiting a compromised website. This link executes a hidden request to a legitimate website where the user is already authenticated.

What Damage Can CSRF Do?

The impact depends on the actions that the targeted web application allows:

1. **Account Takeover:** Attackers can change user passwords or email addresses.
2. **Financial Transactions:** Attackers can make unauthorized purchases or transfers.
3. **Data Manipulation:** Attackers can modify or delete data in the application.
4. **Privilege Escalation:** Attackers can gain administrative privileges if the targeted user is an administrator.

[The thing that makes CSRF scary is that users are completely unaware that they're being attacked. They're just browsing the web as usual, and the malicious action is happening silently in the background.]

Seeing the Bigger Picture: Defense in Depth

These vulnerabilities highlight the importance of a defense-in-depth approach to web application security. No single security measure is foolproof. You need to implement multiple layers of security controls to protect your applications and data.

These basic vulnerabilities highlight the need to test and scan the systems on a regular cadence, as security changes over time. This is the first step in understanding web application vulnerabilities. How can we explore and look at these tools next?

9.2 Web Application Security Testing Techniques: Becoming a Web Application Detective

You've gained an understanding of some common web vulnerabilities. Now, it's time to put on your detective hat and learn how to find these flaws in real-world web applications. This section explores various web application security testing techniques.

The Importance of Testing: Proactive vs. Reactive Security

Security is not a one-time thing. Software updates, patches, and new threat actors mean that the process must always be reviewed and adapted.

- **Manual Testing: The Human Touch**

Manual testing involves manually exploring the web application and looking for potential vulnerabilities. This is the most common way to test code and is a great way to start. There are many nuances that a computer may miss.

1. **Reconnaissance: Know Your Target**
    - **Identify the Application's Functionality:** What does the application do? What are its key features?
    - **Map the Application's Structure:** What are the different pages and sections of the application? How are they linked together?
    - **Identify Input Points:** What are the different ways that users can input data into the application (e.g., forms, URL parameters, cookies)?
    - **Analyze the Technology Stack:** What technologies are used to build the application (e.g., programming languages, frameworks, databases)?
2. **Input Fuzzing: Testing the Boundaries**

    Submit various types of input to different input fields and observe how the application responds. This can help you identify vulnerabilities such as SQL injection, XSS, and buffer overflows.
    For SQLi, use characters that inject code into SQL.
    For XSS, use javascript code to see what can be injected.

3. **Authentication Testing: Breaking into Accounts**

    Test the application's authentication and authorization mechanisms. This involves:

    - **Brute-Forcing Login Forms:** Attempt to crack user passwords using brute-force attacks or dictionary attacks.
      This can be implemented with Hydra.
    - **Bypassing Authentication:** Look for ways to bypass the authentication process, such as SQL injection or session hijacking.
    - **Testing Authorization Controls:** Verify that users are only able to access the resources that they are authorized to access.
4. **Session Management Testing: Hijacking User Sessions**

    Test the application's session management mechanisms. This involves:

    - **Analyzing Session Cookies:** Examine the session cookies to see if they are properly secured (e.g., using the HttpOnly and Secure flags).

    - **Session Fixation Attacks:** Attempt to fixate a user's session by injecting a known session ID into their browser.
    - **Session Hijacking Attacks:** Attempt to steal a user's session cookie and use it to impersonate the user.
5. **Business Logic Testing**

   Business logic flaws occur in how an application handles certain states. An example of these is buying an item in the store for negative money.

[Manual testing is essential for finding complex and subtle vulnerabilities that automated scanners may miss. It requires a deep understanding of web application security principles and a keen eye for detail.]

- **Automated Scanning: The Efficiency Booster**

Automated scanning involves using automated tools to scan the web application for potential vulnerabilities. This can be a faster and more efficient way to find common vulnerabilities.

```
Popular Web Application Scanners:

*   **OWASP ZAP (Zed Attack Proxy):** A free and open-source
web application security scanner that is part of the OWASP
project.
*   **Burp Suite:** A commercial web application security
testing suite that is widely used by professionals.
*   **Nessus:** A commercial vulnerability scanner that can
scan for a wide range of vulnerabilities, including web
application vulnerabilities.
*   **Nikto:** A free and open-source web server scanner that
can detect a variety of common web server misconfigurations
and vulnerabilities.
```

Disclaimer: Always use automated scanners responsibly and ethically. Avoid running aggressive scans that could disrupt the target application.

A Practical Example: Scanning with OWASP ZAP

OWASP ZAP is a powerful and versatile web application security scanner that is easy to use.

1. **Launch OWASP ZAP:**

Open OWASP ZAP from your applications menu.

2. **Configure the Proxy:**

   Configure your web browser to use OWASP ZAP as a proxy. This will allow ZAP to intercept all traffic between your browser and the web application.

3. **Explore the Application:**

   Browse the web application as you normally would. ZAP will automatically record all of the requests and responses.

4. **Run a Scan:**

   Select the target application in the ZAP Sites tree and then click the "Attack" button to run a scan.

   ZAP offers a variety of scan types, including:

   - **Spider:** Crawls the web application to discover all of its pages and resources.
   - **Active Scan:** Sends malicious requests to the web application to test for vulnerabilities.
   - **Passive Scan:** Analyzes the traffic that has already been captured to identify potential vulnerabilities.
5. **Analyze the Results:**

   ZAP will display a list of any vulnerabilities that it finds, along with information about the vulnerability, its impact, and how to fix it.

[Personal Insight Placeholder 2: I've found that automated scanners are a great way to quickly identify common vulnerabilities, but they should not be used as a substitute for manual testing. Automated scanners can miss complex or subtle vulnerabilities that require human insight to detect.]

The Importance of a Combined Approach: Human Intelligence + Automation Power

The most effective approach to web application security testing is to combine manual testing with automated scanning. Manual testing allows you to find complex and subtle vulnerabilities that automated scanners may miss, while automated scanning allows you to quickly identify common vulnerabilities and cover a larger portion of the application.

By using a combined approach, you can maximize your chances of finding all of the vulnerabilities in your web application and ensure that it is secure. What are the most important topics to include here?

9.3 Introduction to OWASP Top Ten: Your Guide to the Web Security Hotlist

You've learned about individual web vulnerabilities and testing techniques. Now, let's zoom out and look at the bigger picture. The OWASP (Open Web Application Security Project) Top Ten is a consensus list of the most critical web application security risks. Think of it as a cheat sheet for understanding the most important threats you need to address.

Why the OWASP Top Ten Matters: Staying Ahead of the Curve

The OWASP Top Ten is a valuable resource because:

- **It's Based on Real-World Data:** The list is compiled based on real-world data about the vulnerabilities that are most frequently exploited in web applications.
- **It's Regularly Updated:** The list is updated regularly to reflect the latest threats and trends.
- **It's a Community Effort:** The OWASP Top Ten is a community-driven project, meaning that it reflects the collective knowledge and experience of security professionals from around the world.
- **It Provides a Common Language:** The OWASP Top Ten provides a common language for discussing web application security risks.
- **It Helps Prioritize Efforts:** By focusing on the OWASP Top Ten, you can prioritize your security efforts and ensure that you are addressing the most critical risks.

The Current OWASP Top Ten: A Rundown (as of the current update cycle):

The OWASP Top Ten list is revised every few years, reflecting changes in the threat landscape. It's important to consult the official OWASP website for the most up-to-date information.

Here's a summary of each entry:

1. **A01:2021 – Broken Access Control:**
   Restrictions on what authenticated users are allowed to do are not properly enforced. Attackers can exploit these flaws to access unauthorized data, functionalities, or administrative parts of the application.
2. **A02:2021 – Cryptographic Failures:**
   Formerly known as "Sensitive Data Exposure," this category focuses on failures related to cryptography. It includes issues like using weak algorithms, improper key management, and failing to encrypt sensitive data in transit and at rest.
3. **A03:2021 – Injection:**
   Injection flaws, such as SQL, NoSQL, OS command, and LDAP injection, occur when untrusted data is sent to an interpreter as part of a command or query. The attacker's malicious data can trick the interpreter into executing unintended commands or accessing data without proper authorization.
4. **A04:2021 – Insecure Design:**
   A new category for 2021, focusing on risks related to missing or ineffective control design. It requires a more holistic approach beyond just individual vulnerabilities, emphasizing the need for secure design patterns and architecture.
5. **A05:2021 – Security Misconfiguration:**
   This includes common misconfigurations such as unnecessary features being enabled, default accounts and passwords, error pages revealing sensitive info, and unpatched vulnerabilities. It's often a result of incomplete or inconsistent configurations.
6. **A06:2021 – Vulnerable and Outdated Components:**
   Using components such as libraries, frameworks, and other software modules with known vulnerabilities. This can expose the application to significant risk if these components are not properly patched or updated.
7. **A07:2021 – Identification and Authentication Failures:**
   Related to failures in identifying users, authenticating them, or managing sessions effectively. It can lead to unauthorized access to user accounts and sensitive data.
8. **A08:2021 – Software and Data Integrity Failures:**
   A new category that includes code and infrastructure that doesn't protect against integrity violations. Examples include using plugins/libraries from untrusted sources, CI/CD pipelines lacking integrity checks, and reliance on software updates.
9. **A09:2021 – Security Logging and Monitoring Failures:**
   Insufficient logging and monitoring of security events can make it difficult to detect, respond to, and recover from active breaches.
10. **A10:2021 – Server-Side Request Forgery (SSRF):**
    A web security vulnerability that allows an attacker to induce the server-side

application to make HTTP requests to an arbitrary domain of the attacker's choosing. In some cases, the attacker can even target internal infrastructure that is behind the firewall from the server-side application.

In General:

This knowledge helps form better threat models for defense planning.

Practical Steps for Addressing the OWASP Top Ten:

1. **Educate Your Team:** Make sure your development team is aware of the OWASP Top Ten and how to prevent these vulnerabilities.
2. **Implement Secure Coding Practices:** Follow secure coding practices to minimize the risk of introducing vulnerabilities into your code.
3. **Perform Regular Security Audits:** Conduct regular security audits to identify potential vulnerabilities in your applications.
4. **Use Automated Security Tools:** Incorporate automated security tools into your development process to help identify vulnerabilities early on.
5. **Stay Up-to-Date:** Stay up-to-date with the latest security threats and trends by subscribing to security mailing lists and newsletters.

[The OWASP Top Ten is a great starting point for building a secure web application, but it's important to remember that it's not a complete solution. You need to implement a comprehensive security program that addresses all aspects of your application's security.]

Putting It Into Practice: Using the OWASP Testing Guide

The OWASP Testing Guide is a comprehensive guide to web application security testing. It provides detailed guidance on how to test for each of the vulnerabilities in the OWASP Top Ten, as well as other common web application security risks.

The OWASP Testing Guide can be used as a reference for both manual testing and automated scanning. It provides a step-by-step approach to testing each vulnerability, along with examples and code snippets.

In Summary:

The OWASP Top Ten is an invaluable resource for understanding the most critical web application security risks. By familiarizing yourself with the OWASP Top Ten and using the OWASP Testing Guide, you can significantly improve the security of your web applications. It can also be used to justify the importance of security and to make a better business case. In what directions can we go?

9.4 Secure Coding Practices: Building Defenses into the Code

You've explored vulnerabilities and learned how to find them. Now, let's shift our focus to prevention. Secure coding practices are the techniques and guidelines that developers should follow to minimize the risk of introducing vulnerabilities into their code. Think of it as building security into the foundation of your applications, rather than trying to bolt it on afterward. Secure software needs to be incorporated into all steps of software development, as well as a good testing step for security.

Why Secure Coding Matters: Prevention is Better Than Cure

Secure coding practices are essential for:

- **Reducing Vulnerabilities:** Preventing vulnerabilities from being introduced into your code in the first place.
- **Improving Security Posture:** Building more secure and resilient applications.
- **Reducing Development Costs:** Fixing vulnerabilities early in the development process is much cheaper and easier than fixing them later on.
- **Protecting Data and Systems:** Protecting your users' data and ensuring the integrity of your systems.
- **Meeting Compliance Requirements:** Meeting regulatory compliance requirements, such as PCI DSS and HIPAA.

Key Principles of Secure Coding:

- **Input Validation:** Validate all user input before processing it.
- **Output Encoding:** Encode all output to prevent malicious code from being injected into your web pages.
- **Authentication and Authorization:** Implement strong authentication and authorization mechanisms to control access to sensitive resources.
- **Session Management:** Securely manage user sessions to prevent session hijacking.
- **Error Handling:** Handle errors gracefully and prevent sensitive information from being exposed in error messages.
- **Least Privilege:** Run the service with least privilege, as is described in Chapter 7.

- **Regular security audits:** Conduct regular security audits to identify potential vulnerabilities

Let's explore these principles in more detail:

1. **Input Validation: Don't Trust Anyone**

   Input validation is the process of verifying that user input is valid and safe before processing it. This is one of the most important secure coding practices, as it can prevent a wide range of vulnerabilities, including SQL injection, XSS, and buffer overflows.

   What to Validate:

   - **Data Type:** Ensure that the input is of the correct data type (e.g., integer, string, email address).
   - **Length:** Ensure that the input is within the expected length range.
   - **Format:** Ensure that the input matches the expected format (e.g., date, phone number, credit card number).
   - **Allowed Characters:** Ensure that the input contains only allowed characters (e.g., alphanumeric characters, specific symbols).
   - **Range:** Ensure that the input is within the expected range of values (e.g., a number between 1 and 100).
2. **Output Encoding: Escaping the Danger**

   Output encoding is the process of converting special characters in user-provided data into a safe format before displaying it on a web page. This prevents malicious code from being injected into the page and executed by the user's browser.

   Different types of output require different encoding techniques:

   - **HTML Encoding:** Used to escape special characters in HTML code, such as <, >, &, ", and '.
   - **JavaScript Encoding:** Used to escape special characters in JavaScript code, such as \, ', ", and newline characters.
   - **URL Encoding:** Used to escape special characters in URLs, such as spaces, <, >, and &.
     You also can encode the information so that if a breach occurs, it will be hard for the attacker to use the details.
3. **Authentication and Authorization: Controlling Access**

Authentication and authorization are essential for protecting sensitive resources and preventing unauthorized access.

- **Authentication:** The process of verifying the identity of a user.
- **Authorization:** The process of determining whether a user has permission to access a specific resource.

Follow these best practices for authentication and authorization:

- **Use Strong Authentication Mechanisms:** Use strong authentication mechanisms, such as multi-factor authentication (MFA), to verify user identities.
- **Enforce Password Policies:** Enforce strong password policies to ensure that users choose passwords that are difficult to guess.
- **Implement Role-Based Access Control (RBAC):** Use RBAC to grant users only the minimum privileges required to perform their tasks.
- **Regularly Review User Privileges:** Regularly review user privileges to ensure that they are still appropriate.

4. **Session Management: Protecting User Sessions**

Session management is the process of tracking user activity across multiple requests. It's important to securely manage user sessions to prevent session hijacking and other attacks.

Follow these best practices for session management:

- **Use Strong Session IDs:** Generate strong, random session IDs that are difficult to guess.
- **Protect Session Cookies:** Protect session cookies by using the HttpOnly and Secure flags.
- **Implement Session Timeouts:** Automatically terminate inactive sessions after a certain period of time.
- **Regenerate Session IDs:** Regenerate session IDs after important events, such as login and password changes.

5. **Error Handling: Don't Reveal Secrets**

Proper error handling is important for both usability and security. When errors occur, it's important to handle them gracefully and prevent sensitive information from being exposed in error messages.

Avoid displaying sensitive information, such as database connection strings or internal file paths, in error messages. Instead, log the error to a secure location and display a generic error message to the user.

[Personal Insight Placeholder 1: I've often seen web applications that leak sensitive information in error messages. This can provide attackers with valuable clues about the application's architecture and configuration.]

Using Frameworks: Leveraging Built-in Security

Many modern web development frameworks provide built-in security features that can help you to implement secure coding practices.

- **Input Validation:** Most frameworks provide built-in mechanisms for validating user input.
- **Output Encoding:** Most frameworks provide built-in mechanisms for encoding output to prevent XSS attacks.
- **Authentication and Authorization:** Most frameworks provide built-in authentication and authorization mechanisms.
- **Session Management:** Most frameworks provide built-in session management features.

Take advantage of these built-in security features to make it easier to build secure web applications.
What is more important? The planning or implementation?
The planning is more important than the implementation. By planning and checking code, much effort can be avoided on the backend.
In Summary:

Secure coding practices are essential for building secure and resilient web applications. By following these practices from the very beginning of the development process, you can significantly reduce the risk of introducing vulnerabilities into your code and protect your users' data. It needs to be a continuous process and not just a once-and-done effort. Any changes made to the system will need to be reviewed and updated to comply with security standards. After making these security choices, what cryptography implementations should we focus on?

Chapter 10: Okay, here's Chapter 10, "Cryptography Fundamentals," crafted to provide a clear and practical understanding of key cryptographic concepts.

Chapter 10: Cryptography Fundamentals: Securing Data with Secret Codes

Cryptography is the art and science of protecting information by transforming it into an unreadable format, called ciphertext. It's the foundation of secure communication, data storage, and digital signatures. Think of cryptography as the toolkit for building secure systems and protecting sensitive information. This chapter explores these fundamental concepts in simple steps.

10.1 Hashing Algorithms: Creating Unique Fingerprints- The One-Way Street of Data Security

In cryptography, a hash function is like a meat grinder. They take data of arbitrary size and produce a fixed-size output (the "hash" or "message digest"). Think of a hashing algorithm as a one-way function that creates a unique fingerprint of your data. It has important qualities that are useful for systems.

- **What Makes a Good Hashing Algorithm? Essential Properties**

  To be useful for security purposes, a hashing algorithm must possess the following properties:

  1. **One-Way (Preimage Resistance):** Given a hash value, it should be computationally infeasible to find the original input that produced that hash. This prevents attackers from recovering passwords from a database of password hashes.
  2. **Deterministic:** The same input should always produce the same hash value. This ensures that you can reliably verify the integrity of data by comparing its hash value before and after transmission or storage.
  3. **Collision Resistance:** It should be computationally infeasible to find two different inputs that produce the same hash value (a collision). This prevents attackers from creating malicious files with the same hash value as a legitimate file.
     There is also Second-Preimage resistance, which means it is hard to find another input that produces the same output.

  A high-quality hashing algorithm is good at all of these factors.

- **Common Use Cases: Where Hashing Shines**

Hashing algorithms are used in a wide range of applications:

- **Password Storage:** Storing passwords securely by hashing them instead of storing them in plain text.
- **Data Integrity:** Verifying the integrity of data by comparing the hash value of the data before and after transmission or storage.
- **Digital Signatures:** Creating digital signatures to verify the authenticity and integrity of digital documents.
- **Message Authentication Codes (MACs):** Creating MACs to verify the authenticity and integrity of messages.
- **Data Structures:** Hash tables and other data structures that rely on hashing algorithms to efficiently store and retrieve data.
- **Proof of Work**: Using the algorithms to check security configurations on many devices that may otherwise not be tested. There are various other methods that are possible with algorithms.

- **Hashing and Salting passwords:**

  This process secures a stored hash of the user's password by modifying the data by adding something else. This modification helps prevent hackers from gaining access in instances like precomputed hash tables.

  You should choose a random salt and keep it secret.

- **Hashing algorithms and keys:**

  Encryption has keys, both public and private. Hashing has a single key. It is important to keep it secured and out of reach for it to be used by attackers. Without the key, no messages can be verified.

Popular Hashing Algorithms: A Tour of the Landscape

Let's take a look at some of the most popular hashing algorithms and their strengths and weaknesses:

- **MD5 (Message Digest Algorithm 5): (Legacy - Do Not Use!)**

  MD5 is an older hashing algorithm that produces a 128-bit hash value. It was once widely used, but it is now considered cryptographically broken due to the discovery of practical collision attacks. This means that it is possible to find two different inputs that produce the same MD5 hash value, making it unsuitable for security-sensitive applications. It is also not collision resistant.

For historical purposes only. Do not use MD5 for new applications.

- **SHA-1 (Secure Hash Algorithm 1): (Legacy - Do Not Use!)**

  SHA-1 is another older hashing algorithm that produces a 160-bit hash value. It was also once widely used, but it is now considered cryptographically weakened due to the discovery of practical collision attacks. It is not collision resistant.

  For historical purposes only. Do not use SHA-1 for new applications.

- **SHA-256 (Secure Hash Algorithm 256-bit): The Current Standard**

  SHA-256 is a more secure hashing algorithm that produces a 256-bit hash value. It is widely used for password storage, data integrity, and digital signatures.

  SHA-256 is generally considered to be a strong hashing algorithm, but it is not immune to attack. As computing power increases, it may become necessary to migrate to even stronger hashing algorithms in the future. There is also SHA-512, which is an acceptable hash for storing keys.

- **SHA-3 (Secure Hash Algorithm 3): The Next Generation**

  SHA-3 is a newer family of hashing algorithms that offer improved security and performance compared to SHA-2. The SHA-3 family includes several different algorithms with different hash sizes, including SHA3-224, SHA3-256, SHA3-384, and SHA3-512.

  SHA-3 is based on a completely different design than SHA-2, making it more resistant to certain types of attacks.
  Keccak is the original. However, SHA-3 is the NIST-approved version of the Keccak.

Practical Implementation: Hashing Files with sha256sum

You can use the sha256sum command on Kali Linux to calculate the SHA-256 hash value of a file:

1. **Open a terminal.**
2. **Run the sha256sum command:**

```
sha256sum myfile.txt
```

Replace myfile.txt with the name of the file you want to hash.

The output will display the SHA-256 hash value of the file, followed by the filename:

```
a8a905534a25ad19c349930bb9998ac9715ddb567a7255b513c006d8f8d2b
56c  myfile.txt
```

You can also incorporate the commands into a bash script.
4. To check multiple files at the same time, add the files after. The bash will iterate through each file to generate a hash.

[Personal Insight Placeholder 1: I always verify the SHA-256 hash value of software downloads before installing them. This helps to ensure that the software has not been tampered with and that it is safe to install.]

Generating a Password Hash

Many languages provide password hashing functions.

- **Python:**

```
    import bcrypt
password = b"secretpassword"
hashed = bcrypt.hashpw(password, bcrypt.gensalt())
print (hashed)
```

Practical Recommendations:

- **Use SHA-256 or SHA-3 for new applications.**
- **Salt your passwords with a unique random value.**
- **Store passwords securely in a dedicated database.**
- **Regularly review your hashing algorithms and update them as needed.**
- **Stay Informed:** Stay up-to-date with the latest research on hashing algorithms and best practices for password storage.

What areas would you like for me to provide examples or further information?

10.2 Symmetric Encryption: The Secret Key- Keeping Secrets with Shared Knowledge

You've learned about hashing, a one-way process. Now, let's explore encryption, which allows you to reversibly transform data into an unreadable format. Symmetric encryption is like having a secret code with a friend: you both use the same key to encode and decode messages.

How Symmetric Encryption Works: A Shared Secret

Symmetric encryption algorithms use the same key for both encryption and decryption. The sender uses the secret key to encrypt the plaintext (readable data) into ciphertext (unreadable data). The receiver uses the same secret key to decrypt the ciphertext back into plaintext. The strength of symmetric encryption rests upon the fact that both sender and receiver are the *only* ones who know the secret key.

This means that if an attacker intercepts the ciphertext without the secret key, they will not be able to decrypt it. The weakness with the method is that if you transfer the password insecurely, then there is a chance for the password to be compromised.

Key Concepts to grasp:

- **Encryption:** The process of transforming plaintext into ciphertext.
- **Decryption:** The process of transforming ciphertext back into plaintext.
- **Key:** The secret value used for both encryption and decryption.

AES (Advanced Encryption Standard): The Gold Standard

AES (Advanced Encryption Standard) is a widely used symmetric encryption algorithm that is considered very secure. It was selected by the U.S. National Institute of Standards and Technology (NIST) as a replacement for the Data Encryption Standard (DES). AES supports key sizes of 128, 192, and 256 bits. The larger the key, the more secure the encryption.

It's important to protect the AES key. Without the key, the data is not useful.

Modes of Operation: Adding Flexibility

AES can be used in different modes of operation, which affect how the algorithm is applied to the data. Some common modes of operation include:

- **CBC (Cipher Block Chaining):** Each block of plaintext is XORed with the previous ciphertext block before being encrypted. This makes the encryption more resistant to certain types of attacks.
- **CTR (Counter Mode):** Each block of plaintext is XORed with a unique keystream generated from a counter. This allows for parallel encryption and decryption, making it faster than CBC mode.
- **GCM (Galois/Counter Mode):** Provides both encryption and authentication, ensuring that the data has not been tampered with. This is generally the preferred mode for new applications.

Practical Implementation: Encrypting Files with openssl

You can use the openssl command to encrypt and decrypt files using AES on Kali Linux.

- **Encryption:**

```
openssl aes-256-cbc -salt -in myfile.txt -out myfile.enc
```

  - aes-256-cbc: Specifies the AES encryption algorithm with a 256-bit key and CBC mode.
  - -salt: Adds a random salt to the password, making it more difficult to crack the encryption. This should always be used, or it might allow an attacker to perform rainbow table attacks.
  - -in myfile.txt: Specifies the input file to be encrypted.
  - -out myfile.enc: Specifies the output file for the encrypted data.

  You will be prompted to enter a password for the encryption key. Choose a strong password and remember it!
  The output of this test will not display information and save to an output file. It is important to have another command running to determine the length of time the algorithm is taking to encrypt.

- **Decryption:**

```
openssl aes-256-cbc -d -in myfile.enc -out
myfile_decrypted.txt
```

  - -d: Specifies that the command should decrypt the data.
  - -in myfile.enc: Specifies the input file to be decrypted.

- -out myfile_decrypted.txt: Specifies the output file for the decrypted data.

You will be prompted to enter the password that you used to encrypt the file. After, run another command to compare the files to see if they are the same.

Challenges and Considerations:

- **Key Management:**

  The biggest challenge with symmetric encryption is key management. You need to securely share the secret key with the recipient of the encrypted data. This can be difficult, especially if the recipient is in a different location or if you need to send the key over an insecure channel.

- **Key Strength:**

  The strength of symmetric encryption depends on the strength of the secret key. Use a strong, random key that is at least 128 bits in length. For increased security, 256-bit keys are typically better.

- **Choosing the Right Mode of Operation:**

  The choice of mode of operation can affect the security and performance of the encryption. GCM mode is generally recommended for new applications as it provides both encryption and authentication.

- **Testing**

There are several ways to test this command to understand how it works. Run encryption without parameters.

- It will then prompt you for password.
- It is helpful to measure performance by adding a timer.
- Check sizes to measure the performance of the resulting size.

I've found that key management is the most challenging aspect of symmetric encryption. It's essential to have a secure process in place for generating, storing, and distributing keys.]

Securely Transferring Keys:

There are several techniques for transferring keys. These will depend on the use case.

*In person handoff*This is the best option but is not always available.
Asymmetric encryption One key is shared to transfer the other.
Quantum Key Distribution This one is hard to implement.

In Summary:

Symmetric encryption is a powerful tool for protecting sensitive data. By understanding the principles of symmetric encryption and using tools like openssl, you can effectively encrypt your data and protect it from unauthorized access. However, it's important to remember that key management is critical. Always use the best tools for your situation! How to best implement encryption?

10.3 Asymmetric Encryption: The Public Key Advantage- Sharing Secrets Without Sharing the Key

You've explored symmetric encryption, where a shared secret key is needed for both encryption and decryption. This creates a challenge: how do you securely share that secret key? Asymmetric encryption provides an elegant solution to this problem by using separate keys for encryption and decryption: a public key and a private key.

How Asymmetric Encryption Works: A Lockbox Analogy

Think of asymmetric encryption like a special mailbox:

- **Public Key:** Everyone has access to the mailbox's slot. Anyone can drop a letter (data) into the slot, encrypting it with the public key.
- **Private Key:** Only the owner of the mailbox has the key to open it and read the letters (decrypt the data).

This means anyone can encrypt a message for you using your public key, but only you can decrypt it using your private key. This solves the key exchange problem inherent in symmetric encryption.

Key Concepts: Understanding the Pieces

- **Public Key:** A key that can be freely distributed to anyone. Used for encrypting messages or verifying digital signatures.

- **Private Key:** A key that must be kept secret and secure. Used for decrypting messages or creating digital signatures.
- **Key Pair:** The public key and private key are mathematically linked, forming a key pair.
- **Encryption:** The process of transforming plaintext into ciphertext using the recipient's public key. Only the holder of the corresponding private key can decrypt the ciphertext.
- **Decryption:** The process of transforming ciphertext back into plaintext using the recipient's private key.

RSA (Rivest-Shamir-Adleman): The Backbone of Secure Communication

RSA is one of the most widely used asymmetric encryption algorithms. It's based on the mathematical properties of prime numbers and is used for secure communication, digital signatures, and key exchange.

- **RSA in Action: HTTPS and More**

  RSA is used extensively in HTTPS (the secure version of HTTP), where it's used to encrypt the communication between your web browser and the web server. It is also used in digital signatures.

- **Practical Implementation: Using openssl**
  It is useful to also check system time to check the differences.

  You can use the openssl command to generate an RSA key pair and encrypt and decrypt files:

  1. **Generate an RSA Key Pair:**

     ```
     openssl genrsa -out private.pem 2048
     ```

     This command generates a 2048-bit RSA private key and saves it to a file named private.pem. You will see the amount of time taken to generate. Keep that file very secured!

     ```
     openssl rsa -in private.pem -outform PEM -pubout -out
     public.pem
     ```

     This command extracts the public key from the private key file and saves it to a file named public.pem. This can be shared.

2. **Encrypt a File:**

```
openssl rsautl -encrypt -inkey public.pem -pubin -in
myfile.txt -out myfile.enc
```

This command encrypts the file myfile.txt using the public key and saves the encrypted data to a file named myfile.enc.

- -encrypt: Specifies that the command should encrypt the data.
- -inkey public.pem: Specifies the public key file to use for encryption.
- -pubin: Indicates that the input key is a public key.
- -in myfile.txt: Specifies the input file to be encrypted.
- -out myfile.enc: Specifies the output file for the encrypted data.

3. **Decrypt a File:**

```
openssl rsautl -decrypt -inkey private.pem -in myfile.enc -
out myfile_decrypted.txt
```

This command decrypts the file myfile.enc using the private key and saves the decrypted data to a file named myfile_decrypted.txt.

- -decrypt: Specifies that the command should decrypt the data.
- -inkey private.pem: Specifies the private key file to use for decryption.
- -in myfile.enc: Specifies the input file to be decrypted.
- -out myfile_decrypted.txt: Specifies the output file for the decrypted data.

This is a good first step to understand it.

Practical Consideration: You can use a tool called GPG to improve security. GPG is a free tool and has the capacity to also manage passwords in a safer manner.

[I've used RSA encryption to secure sensitive data for years. It's a powerful and reliable algorithm, but it's important to follow best practices for key generation and management.]

Key Length: The Security Metric

- For RSA, a key length of 2048 bits or higher is generally recommended. This is needed due to the computation to crack keys.

Key Management: The Biggest Challenge

The biggest challenge with asymmetric encryption is managing the private key. The private key must be kept secret and secure. If an attacker gains access to your private key, they can decrypt all messages that were encrypted with your public key, or forge digital signatures.

- **Protecting Your Private Key:**
    - **Store it Securely:** Store your private key in a secure location, such as an encrypted hard drive or a hardware security module (HSM).
    - **Use a Strong Passphrase:** Protect your private key with a strong passphrase.
    - **Limit Access:** Limit access to your private key to only those who absolutely need it.
    - **Backup Your Key:** Create a backup of your private key in case of data loss or corruption.
- **Public Key Infrastructure (PKI): Trusting the Keys**
  How do you know that the public key you're using to encrypt a message actually belongs to the person you think it does? This is where Public Key Infrastructure (PKI) comes in. PKI is a system for managing and distributing digital certificates, which bind a public key to an identity. There are services to verify digital keys and prevent hackers from changing them without your knowledge.
- Certificates and Certificate Authorities are key pieces to that puzzle.

In Summary:

Asymmetric encryption provides a powerful way to securely communicate and exchange data without having to share a secret key. By understanding the principles of asymmetric encryption and using tools like openssl, you can effectively protect your data and verify the authenticity of digital documents. This area is more complex, so please continue studying other resources!
What is next?

10.4 Digital Signatures: Verifying Authenticity- Your Seal of Approval in the Digital World

You've learned about symmetric and asymmetric encryption for protecting confidentiality. But what about verifying the *authenticity* and *integrity* of data? How can you be sure that a file or message truly came from the person it claims to be from and that it hasn't been tampered with along the way? That's where digital signatures come in. Think of them as the digital equivalent of a handwritten signature, providing assurance about the origin and content of a document.

The Power of Digital Signatures: Trust in a Trustless World

Digital signatures are a cryptographic technique that can be used to:

- **Authentication:** Verify the identity of the sender.
- **Integrity:** Ensure that the data has not been tampered with since it was signed.
- **Non-Repudiation:** Prevent the sender from denying that they signed the document.

These factors help create secure transactions that can have verifiable origins.

How Digital Signatures Work: A Two-Key System

Digital signatures rely on asymmetric cryptography, using a public key and a private key. The process involves:

1. **Hashing:** The sender uses a hashing algorithm (like SHA-256) to create a hash value (a digital fingerprint) of the document or message.
2. **Signing:** The sender encrypts the hash value with their *private key* to create the digital signature. The hash value is just an easy way to test integrity, the whole document can be signed, but it would cost a lot more processing power.
3. **Distribution:** The sender sends the original document or message along with the digital signature.
4. **Verification:** The recipient uses the sender's *public key* to decrypt the digital signature, revealing the original hash value.
5. **Integrity Check:** The recipient independently calculates the hash value of the received document or message using the same hashing algorithm.

6. **Comparison:** The recipient compares the decrypted hash value with the calculated hash value. If they match, the signature is valid, and the document is authentic and has not been tampered with.

Why This Works: The Magic of Asymmetric Crypto

The security of digital signatures relies on the fact that only the owner of the private key can create a valid signature. Anyone with the public key can verify the signature, but they cannot create a new signature or modify an existing one.

Practical Implementation: Using openssl

You can use the openssl command on Kali Linux to create and verify digital signatures.

1. **Generate an RSA Key Pair (if you don't already have one):**

```
openssl genrsa -out private.pem 2048
   openssl rsa -in private.pem -outform PEM -pubout -out
   public.pem
```

2. **Sign a File:**

```
openssl dgst -sha256 -sign private.pem -out myfile.sig
myfile.txt
```

   - dgst -sha256: Specifies that the SHA-256 hashing algorithm should be used.
   - -sign private.pem: Specifies that the private key should be used to sign the hash value.
   - -out myfile.sig: Specifies the output file for the digital signature.
   - myfile.txt: Specifies the file to be signed.
3. **Verify a Signature:**

```
openssl dgst -sha256 -verify public.pem -signature myfile.sig
myfile.txt
```

   - dgst -sha256: Specifies that the SHA-256 hashing algorithm should be used.

- -verify public.pem: Specifies that the public key should be used to verify the signature.
- -signature myfile.sig: Specifies the digital signature file.
- myfile.txt: Specifies the original file.

If the signature is valid, the command will print "Verified OK".

use digital signatures every day to verify the authenticity of software downloads and email messages. It's an essential tool for protecting myself from malware and phishing attacks.]

Hash Algorithm Choice: What's Right for You?

Choose a strong hashing algorithm that is resistant to collision attacks. SHA-256 or SHA-3 are generally recommended. MD5 and SHA-1 are considered cryptographically broken and should not be used.

Practical Applications: Beyond File Verification

Digital signatures are used in a wide variety of applications, including:

- **Software Distribution:** Verifying the authenticity and integrity of software downloads.
- **Email Security:** Signing emails to prove that they came from you and have not been tampered with.
- **Code Signing:** Signing software code to prove that it came from a trusted source.
- **Document Signing:** Signing electronic documents to create legally binding agreements.
- **Blockchain Technology:** Securing transactions and verifying the integrity of the blockchain.

Important Caveats:

- **Key Management:** The security of digital signatures depends on the security of the private key. If the private key is compromised, an attacker can create forged signatures.
- **Certificate Authorities:** In some cases, you may need to rely on a certificate authority (CA) to verify the authenticity of a public key.

Putting It to Practice

You can test by changing one letter of your source file. If the signature check fails, that indicates there is high integrity for your tool.

In Summary:

Digital signatures are a powerful tool for verifying the authenticity and integrity of digital data. By understanding how digital signatures work and using tools like openssl, you can protect your communications, verify the source of your data, and establish a high level of trust within a network. I urge you to continue your research into cryptography and what protections you can implement! Do you have any follow-up questions?

10.5 Using GPG for Encryption & Signing: Securing Your Digital Life, One Key at a Time

You've explored encryption concepts and seen how openssl can be used. Now, let's get practical with GPG (GNU Privacy Guard), a free and open-source tool that puts the power of encryption and digital signatures directly in your hands. Think of it as your personal, portable security fortress.

GPG: Your Privacy Powerhouse

GPG is a complete and free implementation of the OpenPGP standard (RFC 4880). It is not under the control of a company, making it less subject to government regulations. It enables the following actions:

- **Encrypt Messages:** Protect the confidentiality of your emails and files.
- **Sign Messages:** Verify the authenticity and integrity of your emails and files.
- **Manage Keys:** Create, store, and manage your cryptographic keys.
- **Verify Identities:** Verify the identities of other people you communicate with.
- **Automatic security:** The more you are using security tools, the less likely your actions can be observed without proper permissions.

GPG: A Quick Primer on the Terms

Before using, it is key to have a general understanding of security and keys.

- **Key Pair:** A GPG key pair consists of a public key and a private key. These must have been generated by you.

- **Public Key:** Used to encrypt messages for you and verify digital signatures that you have created. You can share your public key with anyone.
- **Private Key:** Used to decrypt messages sent to you and create digital signatures. You must keep your private key secret and secure, as losing this will lead to the keys being unrecoverable.
- **Keyring:** A database that stores your GPG keys and the public keys of other people.
- **Passphrase:** A password used to protect your private key. You will need to enter your passphrase whenever you use your private key.

Step-by-Step: Getting Started with GPG

1. **Install GPG:**

   If GPG is not already installed on your Kali Linux system, you can install it using the following command:

   ```
   sudo apt install gnupg
   ```

2. **Generate a Key Pair:**

   This is the most critical step. This process is for you and only you, so be mindful and secure. To do so, use this command:

   ```
   gpg --gen-key
   ```

   This command will guide you through the process of generating a GPG key pair. You will be prompted to:

   - **Choose a Key Type:** Select the default option (RSA and ECC).
   - **Choose a Key Size:** Select a key size of 2048 bits or higher.
   - **Enter Your Name and Email Address:** It is important to use an email address that you can continue to check, as it is used in your certificate.
   - **Create a Passphrase:** This is required. You will have to store this and if you forget the password, there is no known way to unlock the data.

   The command should take a while to generate the keys, depending on system resources. This is important to generate the keys.

3. **Export Your Public Key:**

   You need to export your public key so that you can share it with other people. To allow import of the encryption to happen, you need to set the armor. You can export your public key using the following command:

   ```
   gpg --armor --export <your_email_address> > public.key
   ```

   Replace <your_email_address> with the email address you used when generating your key pair. Be sure to check to confirm it has been created. Then you have the key. What is next?

4. **List Keys**

   Once you've created the keys, it is important to remember what they look like:

   ```
   gpg --list-keys
   ```

   This will list the key, as well as other imported public keys. It will show the key ID, key size, creation date, and the user ID associated with the key.

5. **Import Key**

   Now we will import a key.

   ```
   gpg --import ./public.key
   gpg --list-keys #You will see the new name
   ```

1. **Encrypt a File:**

   To encrypt a file using GPG, use the following command:

   ```
   gpg -e -r <recipient_email> myfile.txt
   ```

   Replace <recipient_email> with the email address associated with the recipient's public key. This command will encrypt the file myfile.txt using the recipient's public key and create an encrypted file named myfile.txt.gpg.

The system will prompt you for the user of the key. It is important to select the correct key. If it does not exist, then there is a possible concern for safety.

2. **Decrypt a File:**

   To decrypt a file using GPG, use the following command:

   ```
   gpg -d myfile.txt.gpg
   ```

   This command will decrypt the file myfile.txt.gpg using your private key. You will be prompted to enter your passphrase.

3. **Sign a File:**

   To create a detached signature for a file using GPG, use the following command:

   ```
   gpg -b myfile.txt
   ```

   This command will create a detached signature for the file myfile.txt using your private key. The signature will be saved to a file named myfile.txt.sig.

4. **Verify a Signature:**

   To verify a digital signature using GPG, use the following command:

   ```
   gpg --verify myfile.txt.sig myfile.txt
   ```

   This command will verify the digital signature for the file myfile.txt using the sender's public key.

   ```
       #Sample gpg file
   gpg --verify whatever.sig whatever
   gpg: Signature made Sat 16 May 2024 08:57:17 PM UTC
   gpg:                using RSA key <KEY ID>
   gpg: Good signature from "user <user@mail.com>" [ultimate]
   ```

[Personal Insight Placeholder 1: GPG has been an essential tool for me to manage security and privacy. There is some work required to get it running, but the reward is that communications and files will be protected.

It is also important to remember your password. If that is forgotten, then the security is gone.

- **Revoking a Compromised Key:**

What happens if you lose your private key or suspect that it has been compromised? You need to revoke the key to prevent it from being used maliciously.

1. **Create a Revocation Certificate:**

```
gpg --output revoke.asc --gen-revoke <your_email_address>
```

   Replace <your_email_address> with the email address associated with your key pair. This command will generate a revocation certificate and save it to a file named revoke.asc.

2. **Distribute the Revocation Certificate:**

   Distribute the revocation certificate to your contacts and to key servers. This will inform others that your key is no longer valid and should not be used.

You have control of security again.
With this information, you now have all the tools to help secure files.

In Summary:

Cryptography is a fundamental tool for protecting data. By mastering the basic concepts of hashing, symmetric encryption, asymmetric encryption, and digital signatures, you can significantly improve the security of your systems. Remember that this area is always changing and to continue your education on the matter for best practices. Do you want to explore any other aspects of cryptography?

Conclusion

- Next Steps in Your Hacking Journey
- Continuous Learning & Practice
- Ethical Responsibility & Legal Considerations

Appendices

- Appendix A: Kali Linux Tool Reference (Brief Descriptions)

- Appendix B: Common Linux Commands Cheat Sheet
- Appendix C: Resources for Further Learning

www.ingramcontent.com/pod-product-compliance
Lightning Source LLC
LaVergne TN
LVHW080115070326
832902LV00015B/2606